# THE SEVEN DYSFUNCTIONS OF LEADERS

## 21 QUESTIONS TO TRANSFORM YOUR BUSINESS, YOUR CAREER AND YOUR LIFE

**The Seven Dysfunctions of Leaders: 21 questions to transform your business, your career and your life**

Published by Novaro Publishing Ltd,
2 Speedwell Drive, Lindfield, West Sussex, UK
e: publish@novaropublishing.com.

ISBN: 978-1-0685644-0-6

A CIP catalogue record for this book is available from the British Library.

Designed by Chantel Barnett, Clear Design CC Ltd.

For further details about our authors and our titles, see
www.novaropublishing.com.

OLIVIER S. E. COURTOIS

# THE DYSFUNCTIONS OF LEADERS

## 21 QUESTIONS TO TRANSFORM YOUR BUSINESS, YOUR CAREER AND YOUR LIFE

NOVARO PUBLISHING

# CONTENTS

# INTRODUCTION

*'That which does not kill us makes us stronger.'*

**Friedrich Nietzsche,
German philosopher and critic**

Despite all their good intentions, leaders or aspiring leaders can go astray or even off the rails. In doing so, they can have a negative, sometimes irreversible impact on their teams, their organisation and, ultimately, on their careers and their lives. No one is immune. We are all susceptible to reproducing patterns of behaviour or adopting ways of thinking that are contrary to the objectives we wish to achieve.

Without constant vigilance and self-questioning, we risk becoming dysfunctional at any moment. I wanted to summarise over 35 years of professional experience on five continents, and I have grouped my observations into seven dysfunctions.

Lack of self-knowledge can lead you to make the wrong decisions or choose an option for the wrong reasons. Your horizons are limited because you are locked into circles that are too narrow. Your communication is not as effective as you would like. Resources are lacking or exhausted through lack of focus. Inspiration wanes and talent is depleted in the absence of a vision. Lack of confidence creates a climate of psychological insecurity and conflictual situations. In the end, we exhaust ourselves and others, letting too much potential slip away.

These experiences are familiar to us all. It's part of being human and why leadership is such an exceptional gift. I've always been fascinated by the history of organisations: their birth, growth, operation, success and decline. Beyond their particular circumstances, behind their success or failure, there are always human beings and leaders who have been able to influence, drive, act, take charge, imagine, turn ideas into action, sometimes for the better, sometimes for the worse.

This book is about those men and women. It is about you. Whether you are officially in a leadership role or aspire to get one, this book offers you a set of reflections, behaviours, skills, models, practices and tools to recognise the seven potential dysfunctions: for each, there are opportunities and solutions to escape their grasp.

This book is designed so that you can coach yourself, galvanise your teams and organisations, and flourish in your career and your life. Leadership is a muscle we have in us naturally, but one that can only be developed and maintained through regular training.

We are going to examine each dysfunction. The traps you can fall into. The gains you can make by overcoming them. Then the steps you can take to explore and implement your response. In all, we'll ask 21 questions to get you on the right track.

**Beware of alligators**

Some people might think I'm being negative by pointing out the dysfunctional realities facing leaders. I'm convinced that the best way to take advantage of opportunities is to anticipate possible obstacles. I use the metaphor of an alligator to remind us of the need for vigilance.

When you go for a walk in certain parts of Florida, you are warned by road signs of the danger posed by alligators. The aim is to prevent you from falling prey to an irascible or hungry alligator. The aim is not to spoil the party. Forewarned is forearmed.

**Your development journey**

To get the most out of this book, I suggest you take notes as you go along to collect your thoughts, answers and reflections. Here are some of the benefits of using a notebook.

- **Concrete record**: a physical notebook is a tangible record of your thoughts, feelings and experiences. It's a practical reminder of where you've been.

- **Personal space**: your notebook is a safe space where you can openly and honestly express yourself without any judgement.

- **Memory enhancement**: recording your thoughts will help you remember the points of view and details that affect you.

- **Pattern recognition**: over time, you may notice patterns or trends emerging in your thoughts that can provide valuable insights into your behaviour and thought processes.

- **Improved mindfulness**: keeping a journal can help you become more observant and aware in the moment.

**Transform by one percent daily**

The vocation of leaders is not to make others feel better, and even less to take them by the hand. On the contrary, their role is to help others see better, so that they can act better. As an international coach, I have closely observed how leaders deal with challenges: their projects, their objectives, their stakeholders, the context, their careers and their personal lives. Their responses have a profound and lasting impact.

The best results have been achieved by those who have constantly reviewed their way of thinking in order to clarify what actions to take and how to put them into practice. In this respect, let's take inspiration from one of the world's greatest sushi masters, Japanese chef Jiro Ono.

For him, excellence depends on daily action, on continuous improvement, in small steps. His equation is simple: if I mechanically repeat the same gesture every day without being aware of it, after a year I'll be standing still (1). But if I become aware of what I'm doing and improve it by one percent every day, the difference at the end of the year is enormous (37.08). On the other hand, if I slack off a little each day, I quickly reach mediocrity (0.03).

Between 0.03 and 37.08, the choice is easy to make. The aim of this book is to encourage you to aim for continuous improvement in your leadership and behaviour, and to provide you with the tools you need to make one percent progress every day.

# 1

## SELF-IGNORANCE

*'Humanity suffers from an immense introspective deficiency.'*

**Carl Jung, Swiss psychiatrist
and psychotherapist**

*'All the misfortune of men comes from not knowing how to remain at rest in a room.'*

**Blaise Pascal, Swiss mathematician,
physicist, inventor and philosopher**

# SELF-IGNORANCE

**The challenge**: explore who you are with as much energy as you explore the outside world for greater efficiency, greater wellbeing, more constructive relationships and better results.

**The risk**: making the wrong decisions or making decisions for the wrong reasons. Not getting respect. Not respecting yourself. Lack solidity, stability, openness and agility.

**The opportunity**: the clearer, more efficient, more serene and more solid you are in your choices, the more results you achieve and the more confidence you inspire.

**The response**: I suggest we explore the following six questions so you can answer them naturally and instinctively:

- Who am I?

- What drives me to do what I do? (My driving force)

- What am I good at? (My unique talents)

- What really matters to me? (My values)

- What do I bring to the world? What do I contribute? (My contribution, my purpose)

- What are my reinforcing and limiting beliefs?

## The roots of our choices

One day, as I was escorting a Swedish colleague to the airport, she asked me: 'Olivier, what would you say are your strong points?'. A puzzling question for some, but quite normal in our profession and, I confess, amusing at the time. I started spouting off some more or less coherent stuff, which quickly became a stream of adjectives and paraphrases.

'I mean your five main strengths,' she cut me off. The Swedish language seems designed to avoid any circumlocution, even when spoken in English.

That's when things got complicated. In short, one idea leading to another, it is possible to come up with a series of qualities without too much preparation or reflection, but when it comes to condensing them into a clear, complete, coherent and convincing portrait, it requires deeper reflection. We often have an intuitive perception of our qualities and limits, often fragmented, but more rarely conscious and complete.

So, why does self-discovery matter? Throughout our lives and careers, we make decisions. According to some analyses, as many as 35,000 a day, both micro-decisions and ones that transform something in the longer term: a move, a new job, a new relationship, a purchase, a break-up, an investment, a new objective, a new strategy.

These decisions are sometimes conditioned reflexes, decisions taken on automatic pilot, sometimes more or less considered decisions. But even in the latter case, can we really swear that our thinking is enlightened and rational? What motivated me to decide? What explains my hesitation between two or more options? What are my motives for making the right choice? What am I giving up by deciding and will I really be able to live with this renunciation?

These are all legitimate questions. They show just how complex the decision-making process is and how closely linked it is to context, of course, but also to our psychology, our values, our ambitions, our fears and our history. Often much of it is buried, and if not totally unconscious, at least lodged in a grey area that we rarely explore for lack of time, desire or courage.

Yet, if we recognise that our decisions come from deep within us, wouldn't it be a good idea to explore their source? If we want to break out of our conditioned reflex and gain clarity, to gain self-control and ensure better decisions, if we want to break with certain thought patterns and progress, evolve, we need to develop this habit of self-reflection, of questioning ourselves, to bring our self out of its shadow zone and bring clarity to it in full awareness.

Without this continuous effort, we run the risk of repeating poor life or career choices: making purchasing or investment decisions guided by the wrong reasons and producing poor results; judging a situation with the wrong criteria; and taking, or causing our company or our teams to take, the wrong turn. We run the risk of letting ego, anger, fear or laziness steer us in a hazardous direction. To better control our response to events, to gain clarity, serenity and efficiency, we need to better decode the roots of our choices and to put the lie to the adage that the person who knows us least is ourselves. It is never too late to develop the courage for self-exploration and self-questioning.

Self-knowledge also means opening our eyes to the way we interact with others. Everyone we meet in our lives has a way of looking at us, when we first meet them, of course, and even more so with experience. We often prompt the reaction of others. Others are aggressive towards us, perhaps because our attitude provokes them to react violently. We complain about the lack of collaboration of our colleagues, while we may be pushing them into a spiral of competition through our own behaviour. Others avoid telling us what they think because our reaction, when they have done so in the past, has encouraged them to stop taking the risk. The list is endless.

I like to say that it takes two to tango. In any tense or problematic situation, there's me and the other person. If I can't control the other's reaction, I can at least control my own. But I must be aware of my share of responsibility in the interaction.

Parents will recognise the difficulty of establishing an open climate with their teenagers, when the latter are simply responding to their parents' behaviour. Teenagers complain about their parents in turn, while their own behaviour prompts their parents to react in the opposite way to what they would like. It is never too late or too early to learn.

*'If you want to change in small steps, act on your behaviour.
If you want to change in giant steps, act on the paradigms.'*

**Stephen R. Covey,
US author and educator**

## Question 1: who am I?

If I asked you today to answer the question 'who am I?', would you be able to answer spontaneously, or would you need to think about it? Most of us would probably need a little time to think. What could be more normal? But it is a question worth pondering. In a few words, it sums up what drives us in life, what we've accomplished and what we can bring to others in a private or professional context. Being ready to answer it is both a step towards greater self-knowledge and a powerful communication asset during a presentation.

Here's how to get started. Take out your personal notebook. Think of it as your confidant and development partner. On the first page, answer each of the following three questions with a few sentences:

- Who am I? A few sentences about the salient features of your personality, some specific facts about yourself.

- What's my background? A few sentences about your studies, your career and your achievements.

- What are my core competencies? What do I offer? Your services as an individual or as a company.

All on one page. Complex? Probably at first. As the saying goes: give me three minutes and I'll prepare a three-hour presentation. Ask me for a three-minute presentation and I'll need three hours to prepare it. The art lies in condensing your presentation while preserving its essential flavours.

Put the book down. Make a first draft. And come back to it again and again. The process is as valuable, if not more so, than the result. The following questions will help you refine your answers.

## Question 2: what drives me to do what I do? (My driving forces)

You can act your whole life without asking too many questions and for motivation conclude that you have to follow your instincts. And there's some truth in that. As Malcolm Gladwell points out in his book *Blink: The power of thinking without thinking* (Penguin, 2006), our subconscious has stored up a great deal of information that we have buried and, in a way, skipped over during our lives. So much so that, by relying essentially on our conscious knowledge, we deprive ourselves of a large part of our wisdom, our buried experience. Trusting our instincts would therefore, in certain circumstances, offer a more reliable perspective.

But how do we know whether the use of our instincts connects us exclusively to the most relevant information buried deep within us or whether it is not short-circuited by irrelevant or even negative influences? Clarifying the question of our motivations cannot, therefore, bypass our subconscious, but it can at least help us to be clearer about the reasons that drive us to act. When it comes to motivation, there are several models and theories that are useful for identifying the driving forces. Here are two of them.

*McClelland's human motivation theory*

I like this model because of its simplicity. According to McClelland, a 20th-century US psychologist, we all have three categories of essential needs. Their dosage varies from person to person and over time.

- The need for achievement (accomplishment) refers to the drive to accomplish things and succeed, for example, for our life, our family, a business, an exam, a concert, our work, a drawing, a fight or a cake.

- The need for power (status) refers to the drive to have influence over others: your children, family, colleagues, company, circle of friends, networks, city, country or world.

- The need for affiliation (relationships) refers to the need for satisfying social relationships, the need to be accepted, to be part of a group, an undeniable human need even in the loneliest of people.

Using your notebook, reflect on key events in your life or career: first job, graduation, promotion, job change, sabbatical, business start-up, birth of a child, new project. Make a list. Which ones made the biggest impression on you, positively or negatively, on a scale of -5 to +5? Why or why not?

Taking a step back, how did the three needs stated above (achievement, power, affiliation) manifest themselves? Which is more important to you?

Answering this question requires total self-honesty. For example, it is possible that your need for power and influence matters to you, but you reject the idea. In this case, your need is probably in conflict with a value, for example, the value of equality, fraternity or humility. Remember. We are complex beings.

For example, for some of us, the accumulation of medals, trophies and titles is what matters. Is it a need for achievement, a way of gaining recognition for status, a desire to establish your power by wearing the trappings of it? Or a way of being accepted into a group that one respects and admires (affiliation)? Or a combination of two or all three?

This exercise is an iterative process. What became clearer to you as you reviewed your thoughts several times? To make it easier, I recommend that you ask these questions to a few trusted people who know you well. Outside perception is often invaluable and sometimes more accurate than our own. As we said earlier, the exercise of developing self-knowledge requires humility, courage and an open mind.

*Schein's career anchors*

Edgar Schein, who was a professor of organisational development at the MIT Sloan School of Management, suggests that everyone has specific and unique anchor points: each person's perception of their own values, talents, abilities and motivations that form the basis of individual roles and development. We spend the first part of our working lives exploring our specific anchors. As we explore, our boat pulls away from the anchor, and at some point, when the mooring line is fully tensioned, it pulls the boat back to its anchor. To get to know our anchor well, we're advised to seize every opportunity to explore, to speed up the process of discovery and to better understand what we're made for. Schein identified the following anchors:

- **Technical/functional competence**: these people like to excel at specific tasks and work hard to develop the specific skills needed to accomplish them.

- **General management skills:** these people thrive in a position of responsibility, tackling high-level problems, building relationships and interacting with others; they need strong emotional intelligence skills to succeed.

- **Autonomy/independence:** these people need to be left to their own devices and to be able to act without needing too much direction, interference or confirmation, often eschewing norms and procedures to do things their way.

- **Security/stability:** these people are looking for stable, predictable jobs and activities, around which they can plan certain aspects of their lives, taking few risks; they are also often people who spend many years in the same job.

- **Entrepreneurial:** these are the creatives within a company, who enjoy brainstorming and inventing new things, and often seek to run or launch their own business; they are different from those who seek autonomy, as they share the workload with others and appreciate individuals taking ownership of their work; they are often bored and seek financial gain.

- **Service/dedication to a cause:** these people are always looking for new ways to help others, both inside and outside the organisation, using their talents; they are often found in relevant areas of employment, such as human resources and customer service.

- **Pure challenge**: these people are almost entirely motivated by the need to be constantly stimulated by new challenges and tasks that test their problem-solving abilities; they often seek to change jobs when their current position stagnates, or they no longer have the challenges they need to progress.

- **Lifestyle**: these people orient everything, including their role, around their overall lifestyle. It is not so much about balancing work and life as integrating them; they may also take long periods off to participate in recreational activities or balance themselves and their lives through vacations and other forms of down time.

Schein explains that we all have an anchor point. For example, we may find ourselves managing a team, even though our anchor is not managerial but, for example, pure challenge. This will not prevent us from doing a good job as managers, as long as pure challenge remains at the heart of our daily lives. Otherwise, we risk neglecting our managerial obligations and looking for tasks that better meet our expectations of challenge. Obviously, a manager with general management skills as their anchor will be better equipped to remain committed and carry out their managerial duties effectively.

Another example: a self-employed person driven by autonomy/independence, who starts up a business but has difficulty developing it, because they struggle to delegate.

They can work on their management skills, but, if their real motivation is autonomy/independence, they will have to discipline themselves to manage their teams. Many of us aspire to a pleasant lifestyle, but when you have lifestyle as your anchor, you organise your life around this anchor over the long term.

Using your notebook, review the eight anchors and make your own assessment, giving each one a score from one to nine.

Human beings are complex. They are made of tectonic plates that often move in opposite directions. So it is pointless to look for a clear, absolute answer to any question about ourselves. If the results are disparate or even contradictory, there's nothing to worry about. But try to identify strong tendencies. And identify your anchor. According to Schein, there's only one. To help you in this process, take a look at the previous exercise, in which you were asked to describe yourself in one page. Does this description give you any clues about your potential anchor?

**Question 3: what am I good at? (Strong points)**

What's the point of striving to develop your weaknesses and neglecting your strengths, taking them for granted and forgetting to bring them to the highest level of excellence? Why not reverse the equation? Build your life on your natural strengths, thus releasing energy in your preferred areas and reserve the remaining energy to work on a few weak points that are essential to your success, bringing them to an acceptable level where they no longer constitute a risk or an obstacle. It requires courage and clear-sightedness.

Unfortunately, I've met leaders who burn up their energy by persisting in a path or mission that doesn't suit them, just to prove to themselves that they can do it. Perseverance is a quality, but when it turns into obstinacy, it becomes a major obstacle to efficiency and career development. Sometimes you must let go in time, admit your limitations and move on. Every minute spent doing something that others could do better, instead of focusing on something that corresponds to a natural strength, is a missed opportunity for systemic optimisation on the one hand and personal excellence on the other.

The question of strengths is an inherent part of self-discovery. To put it simply, a strength is something you enjoy doing and do well. It is hard to excel at something you hate doing. It is true that you can improve, but you'll always lack the extra energy, the zest of inspiration that allows you to surpass yourself in the long term. Conversely, it is hard to love something you do badly or something that costs you more energy than others, because you're simply not cut out for it. I've seen leaders build entire careers against nature. It comes at a price.

A strong point, a talent, can be expressed in many different ways. It can be a quality, such as perseverance; a field, such as sales; a behavioural or functional skill like coaching or financial analysis; an activity, such as the development of new services; or an environment, such as the scientific world or the Latin regions.

Take out your notebook and ask yourself the following questions:

- What do I really like to do and do well?

- Where do I tend to spend more time than necessary once I get going (often a telltale sign)?

- At the expense of what else?

- Where do I tend to procrastinate?

- Are there opportunities to focus more on the activities on which I naturally concentrate?

- What can I do about the activities I tend to put off or neglect? What do I really want to do more of?

- What should I entrust to others?

- What's stopping me?

- What have I developed most naturally so far?

- How do others perceive my strengths? my weaknesses?

- What does this mean?

- Why not ask them in person or in writing?

I remember a colleague who sent me an email a few years ago, saying in essence: 'hello, Olivier, as part of an exercise to reflect on my career, I'd appreciate it if you could honestly answer the following question: what do you think are my most visible and indisputable strengths? what would you recommend I do to consolidate them? An ambitious, courageous and humble approach.

## Question 4: what really matters to me? (My values)

We are guided in life by an invisible hand that makes us act and react in a certain way: our values. Values are relative and personal. I remember many years ago, in 1987 to be exact, when I visited New York for the first time. At the time, it was a city with a reputation for being dangerous and tough from a European point of view. People were advised to avoid the subway at all costs, as it was considered a hotbed of crime. So, I decided to take the subway, in search of a thrill and immersion in New York reality and, incidentally, a quick and convenient way to get to the Staten Island ferry.

In the muggy heat of a fine September day, as we stood in line to buy a ticket, a homeless man came up to us and begged for a few dollars. Apparently without much success. When he reached the lady in front of us, he insisted and the woman replied aggressively, 'get a job man'. A harsh retort from a European point of view, but perfectly acceptable in the United States. The values of self-help and individual charity are probably more deeply rooted there than in Europe, where we generally rely on the state to help, but the values of individual responsibility and hard work take precedence over everything else. Was this person heartless and egocentric? Perhaps from a European point of view. Not necessarily from an American standpoint. It's about your hierarchy of values.

Values are a powerful and relatively stable driving force. They are deeply rooted and don't change so easily. And why change them? They differ from beliefs, which are more superficial and subject to change. Understanding our values is essential, because they drive everything we think and do, shaping our environment in their image.

As a leader, whether as a parent, influencer, executive, entrepreneur or chief medical officer, we consciously or unconsciously impose our own values on those around us. They are powerful, sometimes serving our objectives, sometimes getting in the way. Business partners may be driven by a common ambition, yet part ways based on divergent values.

Values sometimes conflict with each other. Your values may include honesty and opportunism and, when faced with certain opportunities, you may put honesty first, whereas someone else with the same values may put opportunity before honesty.

Sometimes values conflict with compelling needs. We may consider honesty a key value and steal food because we're hungry. Others may prefer to beg. That's why you read in the news about a homeless person who brings in a large sum of money found on the street, while others would pocket it and see it as an opportunity to get out of their misery.

You can be on the verge of exhaustion but work yourself to death because you consider keeping your commitments to be more important than anything else. Or working as a salaried employee to pay the bills while having independence and entrepreneurship as core values. Values and needs therefore clash in a multitude of highly personal combinations.

Take out your development notebook and reflect on the key decisions you've made in your life, such as your studies, relationships, children and career. Write down a few of them. You can add to them later.

- What guided you?

- What values led you to make these choices?

- If you've reacted strongly to a situation, what values were torpedoed in that situation and provoked your reaction?

- What are you most revolted by?

- Why?

- Taking a step back, what seems clearer about your values?

- What conclusions can you draw?

**Question 5: what do I bring to the world? what do I contribute? (My contribution, my purpose)**

The Japanese have a word that sums up the question of purpose: *ikigai* (pronounced ee-kee-guy), a life worth living, from *iki* meaning life or living and *gai* meaning value or worthwhile. According to this philosophy, happiness means spending most of your time on an activity that is meaningful to you. In essence, a reason to get up in the morning that makes sense and makes you want to.

There's also a lot of talk about the concept of purpose: a reason for living that lifts up ourselves and others. I've had the opportunity to help many leaders reflect on their purpose. It is true that the more we are aware of our raison d'être, the clearer and more serene our choices. We all have a true north. Becoming fully aware of it, and putting our finger on it, frees up our energies, enabling us to act with greater confidence and serenity, gaining in coherence and gravitas. In short, it acts like a compass. Without it, we're dependent on the stopwatch. You flail about like a pirouette in the wind.

If you're lucky, the winds blow northwards. But if they turn south, you're swept along by the headwinds, and you move forward with the consistency of a feather in a hurricane. Awareness of your north enables you to ride out the adverse winds and stay the course, come what may. Others call it the why.

So let's explore what it means for you as a leader. In your notebook, make a note of the five most important of your unique talents (see question 3). Do the same with your values (question 4). Choose your top five.

Your purpose consists of putting your talents to work (for example, strategic sense, emotional intelligence, knowledge of the financial world) in the service of your values, (for example, equality, professional success, continuous development) in order to, for example, bring the truth to my contemporaries, if you're a journalist, or build a fairer society or create affordable housing for as many people as possible. Although it might seem heavy, this sentence can be refined over time and become your most valuable ally in your life and career development. Combined with your description (question 1: who am I?), you have a compass and a solid communication tool.

**Question 6: what are my reinforcing and limiting beliefs?**

This brings us to beliefs, also known as paradigms. So how do they differ from values? There are many definitions. To put it simply, while both govern our thoughts and behaviour, the main difference is that values are principles, ideals or standards of behaviour, while beliefs are convictions, we hold to be true. A bit like a mainstream (our values) that drives us in one direction, and incessant interferences (our beliefs) that can act as counterstreams in some cases.

Examples of values include loyalty, courage, compassion and respect. We may consider them indispensable and prioritise them in a highly personal way. They come from our upbringing, our environment, our character, our personality, and they induce a series of norms, ways of doing or thinking. They may change with age and experience, but they generally form a stable and enduring foundation.

Beliefs can be derived from values. But they can also develop from a series of limited experiences or through copy-and-paste mimicry or social convenience. For example: 'never trust a ...', 'people in such and such a place are all ...', 'never share your motivations out loud', 'leaders must accept making themselves vulnerable by being honest about their weak points', 'leaders must never make themselves vulnerable'. They can also be found in sayings such as 'never put off until tomorrow what you can do today' or 'look after your horse if you want to go far'.

In this respect, I recall a positive feedback exercise with a group of managers in Saudi Arabia. After a while, one of the managers admitted to me that the exercise was strange. On the one hand, they were enjoying the exercise, on the other they were struggling with a belief ingrained in their culture that you have to be wary of any flatterer. In short, as you can see, beliefs can be based on lifelong experience (not always our own) or on a simple clue. They can change according to events or remain fixed forever. They can be useful for saving time, but they can clutter up our minds, like old objects gathering dust in an attic, and hinder our freedom of thought without us necessarily being aware of it.

Intuitively and personally, I've always considered values to be respectable because they constitute a personal, coherent, universally applicable foundation, whereas beliefs creep in without warning and don't always stand up to the test of truth. They are usually convictions, rarely considerations.

In any case, proven or not, our beliefs can be useful when they strengthen us, but toxic when they limit us.

I am reminded of a young French executive who spent several years at McKinsey & Co, before taking on a management role in a fast-growing company. Her long-held belief was that, since she hadn't been to France's *grandes écoles*, she'd never land a big job. It could have become a limiting belief, but fortunately for her, life's events and her determination enabled her to shed these limiting beliefs and replace them with new ones that enabled her to climb the ladder and become a successful executive.

Spontaneously, write down a series of beliefs that are hindering your progress. Beliefs about yourself, about your failures and successes, about your career, your teams, your partners, your projects, your organisation, your life. Don't stop. After a while, reread them and consider each one.

- Where do they come from?

- What are they based on?

- Can they stand up to the test of truth?

- Do they help you live your *ikigai*, satisfy your needs, harness and develop your talents, express your values?

- Are they your best allies or your worst enemies? in the latter case, why hold on to them?

Write down five beliefs you want to eliminate from your world today: think of the release you'll feel. What can you accomplish without them?

## Conclusion

You can live happily in ignorance. Yet curiosity is the indispensable ally of any leader who wants to progress. A boundless curiosity that drives us to explore unknown territories. Strangely enough, we explore the vast outside world more easily and spontaneously than we explore ourselves.

As the saying goes: 'they wanted to change the world, but couldn't. Then, they tried to change their country, but failed. They tried to change their city, but to no avail. Finally, they decided to change themselves, and they realised, a little too late, that if they had started with themselves, they would have been better able to change their city, then their country, then the world'.

Moral of the story: work on yourself as early as possible and continue to update your software throughout your life. It is the key to a fulfilled life and to successful leadership.

# 2

## ISOLATION

*'Be bold. Step out of your comfort zone, burn stereotypes, labels, categories, and build community.'*

**Kaylee Stepkoski, adventure writer**

*'Building bridges goes further than building walls.'*

**DaShanne Stokes, commentator and activist**

## ISOLATION

**The challenge**: building bridges between stakeholders to generate added value and win-win agreements.

**The risk**: getting stuck in too narrow a circle, disconnecting from realities and weak signals. Lacking information, inspiration and creativity. Acting in an egocentric or one-sided way. Impoverishing yourself materially, spiritually and intellectually.

**The opportunity**: building bridges, developing constructive and productive relationships. Gaining a broad, diversified perspective. Optimising your networks. Activating collective intelligence. Win-win thinking and action.

**The response**: in seeking to make our daily one percent improvement, let us ask two questions:

- Who do I spend most of my time with?
- What is my balance point between ego and generosity?

**Creating links to create value**

Travel shapes youth. When you think about it, where does this phrase come from? Pause for a moment, close your eyes and ask yourself these two questions: have I experienced this personally, and, if so, how did these journeys shape me? As a saying, it recalls two diverging moments in a young person's life.

First, the child becomes an adolescent. Adolescence is the time of life when we rebel, explore our bodies, often taking risks with them, and search for our identity. In this quest, we get closer to those who resemble us or with whom we identify. This leads to a form of mimicry and conformity to the group in question, often in opposition to others.

When we travel, we experience the opposite. Travel is a way out of this confinement. It forces us to see things differently, to meet people who think, act, behave and speak differently. It confronts us with ourselves, with our solitude. This discovery, especially when travelling alone, acts as an electroshock. It forces us to break codes and ask questions. In this respect, travel is highly formative. Adolescents are confronted with this human paradox: on the one hand, the need for certainty and belonging to a community or group, and, on the other, the need to break the shackles and take every liberty.

Some adults are always on a quest, while some teenagers lock themselves in at an early age. Many spend their lives in their clan, their territory, their certainties, and never move from there. To each his own rhythm, to each his own path.

At the heart of it all, there's the opportunity to expand our narrow horizons, to exercise that muscle while it is still supple. Otherwise, there's a risk of ankylosis, the risk of remaining locked into certain patterns of thought and action if we don't question ourselves regularly. The more experience you gain, the greater the risk of entrenchment. 'I've always acted like this, I don't see why I should change.' It is a regrettable risk, especially when you aspire to develop your leadership skills.

I recall a participant in a management training course I ran at the start of my career, a civil servant in a large government department, who confided to me over lunch: 'I've spent many years building up my balance, I am not going to risk upsetting it now'. As the saying goes, you can stop living at 40 and die at 80.

Let's look at another situation for a moment. Your curiosity drives you to surf the net. You have your own media, your own favourite sites. One day, you click on a link to consult a proposal for a trip to Florence, Italy. After a few minutes, you close the site and go back to what you were doing. One phone call later, you've completely forgotten the image of the Ponte Vecchio and the rafting cruise on the Arno. Yet, as you're cruising along, you'll receive an email reminder: there's still time to take advantage of the €180 room. Curiously, later on, other apps will suggest articles on Tuscany, Italian publications, vlogs and other literature. That's the power of algorithms. Thanks to them, you'll find other sources of useful information that you might otherwise have missed.

The danger is getting locked into a loop. If you have a certain inclination in favour of one thesis, the algorithms will suggest content that will reinforce your initial view. You're going to need a lot of willpower and insight to explore divergent points of view and break the loop. Today's social media and their algorithms tend to lock people into a single mode of thought based on their initial sensitivity, offering them a sounding board and a network of allies. We find ourselves locked in circles, in loops, and we no longer have the opportunity, the desire, the curiosity or the presence of mind, to click on something else, to try and understand other points of view or the position of the opposing party.

Now, the leader can ride this wave and bring like-minded people with them against another group. But leadership is also about bringing different people together, building bridges, including them in a common project that transcends differences. As a leader, you will be wary of algorithms for yourself and your teams. Or at least be aware of what they represent.

Algorithms are also at work in real life. When you belong to the same circles, listen to the same people, join the same clubs, you always end up with a biased, narrow vision of reality. We are reinforced by the convictions, rituals and conventions of these groups. In a way, we all live in our own bubbles. That's why it is important to consciously step outside. As adults, we have the privilege of having resolved the question of identity, at least to a large extent. So, opening up to others shouldn't call into question who we are. In principle, that is.

Many years ago, I remember coming across a book entitled *L'art de réussir sans travailler* (*The art of succeeding without working*), the exact details of which escape me. I apologise to the author. He wrote under a pseudonym and presented himself as an executive who wanted to denounce the life and rituals of large groups, in this case French. For example, in the off-peak hours of the afternoon, he suggested going to the movies or for a stroll around town, leaving your jacket on the back of the chair, taking a few documents under your arm, walking briskly as if from one meeting to another. No one would notice, he suggested. Of course, in the evening, you wouldn't want to miss your superior's 'good evening', so you'd have to wait patiently for him to leave, and then turn everything off ten minutes later.

A book from another time, and of course provocative. A humorous book to be read in the second degree. But it forces us to step outside our algorithms and ask ourselves a series of good questions about the meaning of work, our way of working and organising our time. A sort of 1980s version of quiet quitting.

I lent this book to a neighbour, a workaholic on the rise, just to cheer him up a bit. He never read it. I found it fascinating. I sensed a reluctance on his part to take the risk of exploring a different universe for fear of being contaminated by the subversive ideas of a dangerous tempter, in this case his neighbour. I respect his choice, of course, but in my opinion, it is illustrative of the difficulty some have in listening, in opening up to others, to those who live differently, for fear of being shaken in their foundations or beliefs. A capital sin for a leader.

There's nothing simpler, as keynote speaker Lars Sudmann tells his audiences, than clicking on anything and everything. After a while, something new will come up, perhaps the start of a new inspiration, a new holiday or business idea.

I'd add in real life, click at random too. Always set aside a moment to get off the beaten track, literally and figuratively, physically and intellectually. This exercise requires regular practice to keep the muscles of openness and curiosity supple. Because your ability to innovate, to include, to inspire, to challenge yourself, to evolve and to strengthen yourself depends on it.

Building bridges is at the heart of wealth creation. It generates material, spiritual, intellectual wealth. The quality and scope of your networks will play a major role in your potential for success, whatever your goal. And here we come back to our algorithms. The vagaries of life, our immediate needs, our conscious or unconscious preferences, our beliefs (limiting or reinforcing), our fears whether of failure, ridicule, imposter syndrome or social conditioning, will determine the nature and extent of our networks. As a future leader, it is essential to manage our networks consciously and purposefully. It is not a question of calculating everything in our relationships, but of regularly re-evaluating our networking to optimise our approach.

**Question 7: who do I spend most of my time with?**

We are the average of the five people closest to us, according to Jim Rohn, the US motivational author and speaker. No doubt because of the social mimicry that no one can escape. Experiments have demonstrated the driving force of the group with which we identify. In certain poor communities in Central America, for example, the social ascent of a single member of the community, thanks to the implementation of work methods proposed by support organisations, has a ripple effect on the other members of the community. Returning to teenagers, the type of people they rub shoulders with will often have more influence than the preaching of their parents or educators.

If we're ambitious, we'll move closer to an urban centre, to have more opportunities to meet people like ourselves, to widen our circles of influence and exchange, which will affect our way of seeing things, our perceptions of what's possible or desirable. An entrepreneur will find support and inspiration in a community of entrepreneurs or a business hive. When we're born into and rub shoulders with wealthy, enterprising people, we naturally mimic their ways of thinking and acting.

We are therefore strongly influenced by the people with whom we are most in contact. We also naturally seek out people who enrich and complement us. This opens up new horizons for us but can also reinforce the dynamic of confinement. So, we need to remain vigilant.

In your notebook, write down the people or categories of people you spend the most time with.

- What do you make of this list?

- Is it by choice, natural inclination or obligation?

- Are you satisfied?

- Do these people enrich you, make you grow, push you to excel?

- Do they give you confidence?

- Do they open your mind?

- Do they open doors for you?

- What do you bring to them?

- What would they say about you if your name appeared in their personal development book?

- What are you looking for from these people: support? recognition? to be challenged? to help you think? reassurance? favours? information? reputation?

If you manage teams, or plan to do so, these questions are even more critical. First, there's the question of balance.

- Do you spend as much time with each member of the team (replace the word team with executive committee if you're chief executive).

- If not, why not?

- Have you considered the perceptions of different team members?

- And what about the rest of the organisation?

- What do your individual relationships with each team member say about you, your plans, your leadership?

- Are they likely to strengthen cohesion, trust or commitment or not?

Then there's the question of openness.

- Do you reserve your time and energy for a few people in a close circle? Or do you open up your relationships to other people or circles?

- Who are these people?

- What are these circles?

- Are these circles inside or outside your organisation?

- Are they consistent with your longer-term goals and ambitions?

- Are there any people or categories of people you need to remove from or add to the list?

## Question 8: what is my balance point between ego and generosity?

Leadership involves reconciling a paradox. On the one hand, it is difficult to emerge as a leader, to generate the energy and motivation needed to influence and lead others without a healthy dose of ego. On the other hand, an excessive ego will prevent an emotional connection with others, which, I'm sure you'll agree isn't a good start if you want to create commitment and trust. I've observed that effective leadership always relies on a balance between ego, the self-centred, and generosity, focused on the needs of others.

*Ego*

It all starts with ego and personal ambition. To say the least, the concept of ambition is controversial. Some definitions have a clearly negative connotation: ambition is 'the desire for glory, for social success, for anything that honours your self-esteem'. Alternatively, it is 'the sin by which we seek honour in a disordered way'. Sometimes we see a more positive undertone: 'desire to accomplish, to achieve a great thing, by committing your pride, your honour' or 'human action has the inevitable ambition to define and realise within itself this idea of perfection'.

In some instances, it becomes more ambiguous: what does excessive ambition mean? Does excessive define a type of ambition or is it associated with all types of ambition?

You also see: generous ambition, great ambition, heroic ambition, legitimate ambition, praiseworthy ambition. Here ambition seems acceptable if is accompanied by a meliorative adjective.

In any case, the word carries many connotations. I personally take it in its most positive sense coupled with the word generosity. There can be no leadership without a certain will to power and influence. Gandhi, Mother Teresa and Mandela were not without it. Far from it. Leadership implies knowing what you want, having personal ambition, egocentric to a certain extent, and being comfortable with that ambition. I take issue with the criticism levelled at politicians, or leaders in general, that they are power-hungry and have overinflated egos. Fortunately, I'd like to say, there are human beings who enjoy having power.

Those who criticise are often no less sensitive to the attractions of power in their own context. The problem is not power itself. Nor is it that we enjoy having it. The question is what to do with it? What do we try to get with it?

*Generosity*

Ego, ambition and the will to power, essential drivers of leadership, must be accompanied by a large dose of generosity to develop a leadership posture: a generous person, who has a big heart, who shows high feelings of devotion, of self-forgetfulness, who gives of themself to others, their family, their neighbours, their city, their country, a human group or a cause, automatically has a purpose and an audience. Generosity is the purpose of all human endeavours and all human life. It is where the material and the spiritual meet.

Prosperity can only come from bringing value to others. The world only makes sense in exchange with others. If my egocentric ambition drives me to develop and offer a service or product that is of no interest to anyone, no matter how hard I try, at the end of the day I'll have no choice but to starve or beg. My survival, my prosperity, my happiness depend solely on my ability to bring something of value to others.

To develop leadership skills, ego and generosity must coexist. Because generosity alone does not automatically transform its author into Gandhi or Mother Teresa. Thousands of people found British colonisation of India revolting, but only a few were ambitious enough to tackle the situation. Many people are revolted by poverty, some make donations, some help on the side, but few have the ambition to devote their lives to transforming the situation on a large scale. To do that, you need ambition.

Of course, the human value of a leader cannot be measured by their level of ambition and generosity. Every commitment is respectable and not everyone has the same talent or the same opportunities. Luck will also play its own part. You can do all you want and all you can do, but luck and destiny have their part to play. It takes two to tango. You should never blame yourself for not reaching the level you were aiming for. On the other hand, you must try and do what you can on your own with ambition and generosity.

In business, however, the value of a leader is often measured in dollars, pounds, euros, yen or yuan as indicator of their ability to transform available energy into added value.

Let me suggest the following reflection:

- What is your ambition for the next five years? The five-year timeframe is arbitrary and you may decide to shorten it to two or three years. However, I would advise against too long a timeframe, which would dilute the benefits of the exercise. Describe your ambition in no more than one sentence. For example: 'become a manager in my field of activity in my current company or elsewhere', 'get my degree and move to Asia', 'become chief executive', 'create a foundation', 'enter the top three' or 'have a fortune of x thousands'.

- From this ambition, you will now define three pillars that will form the basis of your action plan. For example, if your ambition is to become chief executive, you might have as pillars: clarify my purpose, consolidate growth in my current role and stakeholder management. If your ambition is to consolidate your wealth, you could choose as pillars: start an investment plan, develop my financial knowledge and join a community of investors. You've got the idea.

- Then for each pillar, define two steps. For example, if your pillar is to develop your knowledge, step 1 could be to read and take online courses and step 2 to consolidate by subscribing to specialist magazines and joining a club. These steps can be arranged in chronological order, or as two separate, parallel sub-pillars, depending on your needs.

- Finally, the activities section allows you to move on to concrete actions. List a series of concrete actions for each stage. You can concentrate on one pillar or step for a certain period of time, then move on to another or operate in parallel. As you can see, the further to the right you are on the chart, the more evolutionary the space is and the more frequently you need to update it.

| Ambition | Pillar 1 | Step 1 | Activities |
|---|---|---|---|
|  |  | Step 2 |  |
|  | Pillar 2 | Step 1 |  |
|  |  | Step 2 |  |
|  | Pillar 3 | Step 1 |  |
|  |  | Step 2 |  |

*Exercise: a plan to make ambitions happen*

Once the exercise is complete, all that remains is to implement the roadmap and update it regularly. To this end, ask yourself: does my action plan balance my ambition with the opportunity to demonstrate my generosity to bring added value in the form of time, energy and tangible resources?

## Conclusion

The first military reflex when isolating an area is to destroy existing bridges. Conversely, building bridges brings people and territories closer together. The same is true on a personal level. When a relationship becomes toxic or impoverishing, we cut the bridges.

Leadership is about building bridges. Between yourself and others, and between different people or categories of people. Clearly, building bridges must be a conscious, deliberate process. The development of constructive relationships is too important to be left to chance. As a leader, our ability to build bridges is not only intrinsic to our position, it will also serve as an example to others and produce a ripple effect.

However, I'd also like to stress the value of authenticity and spontaneity. You can aim to build bridges voluntarily and consciously without necessarily appearing to be purely opportunistic. There's nothing more unpleasant and often counterproductive than dealing with a pure opportunist for whom everything is calculated. We can all think of those people who ignore you royally until the day they need you. In this respect, it is important to maintain relationships without expecting automatic or immediate reciprocity. Productive exchanges must be fluid, graceful and elegant. It's part of your personal brand as a leader.

# 3

# POOR COMMUNICATION

*'In the beginning was the Word.'*

**Gospel according to St John**

*'The art of communication is the language of leadership.'*

**James C. Humes, US author and
former presidential speechwriter**

# POOR COMMUNICATION

**The challenge**: connect, touch, inspire people and achieve your objectives through impactful communication.

**The risk**: creating barriers with stakeholders. Confusion due to lack of clarity or consistency. Getting lost in monologues. Making too much noise. Not being heard properly. Conveying a bad image.

**The opportunity**: rally people around a cause, a vision, a project through an engaging story. Inspire. Convince. Create trust. Clarify. Get results.

**The response**: improve your communication by asking three questions.

- What stories do I tell?
- Who do I communicate with?
- How do I communicate?

## The cornerstone of collective achievement

Deep in the African forest were two monkeys. The first, starving, noticed that the second had bananas. 'I'll have a banana', he thought. So, he tried to approach the second monkey, trying to make him understand the deal he wanted to offer: 'give me one banana and tomorrow I'll give you two back'. Obviously, his limited language didn't allow him to convey all the nuances necessary for the credibility of the message, and the other monkey only understands one thing: a monkey wants to take my banana, he thinks I am a moron. A fight or retreat ensues.

A few hours away, in a gleaming tower block in Kigali's business district, an educated, elegant man in a three-piece suit proposes the following deal to a fellow human being in sophisticated language: 'give me this sum of money, and in exchange, I'll give you some crypto. Tomorrow you'll be rich, let me explain ...'. The fellow starts dreaming and accepts the deal.

Who's the wiser in all this? The ape who only believes what he sees or the imaginative human? In his remarkable book *Sapiens*, Yuval Noah Harari (Vintage, 2015) explains that complex human societies developed thanks to language. It is language that has enabled us to imagine and make promises of a brighter tomorrow. Equipped with language, humans were able to obtain the attention, efforts, resources, loyalty and commitment of their fellow human beings or disciples in exchange for the promise of a better world. It was through language that empires, nations and religions were born. It is remarkable that millennia ago, empires were built without sophisticated and rapid means of communication, simply by circulating stories, promises of a better world. This won the loyalty of armies and the support of citizens thousands of miles away. The capacity for communication and reflection offered by language has enabled the development of great civilisations, the conclusion of fruitful agreements, but also the exploitation of the gullible by those with knowledge.

The leader is the one who gains the attention or resources of others through effective communication. Of course, good communication that fails to deliver on its promise will be considered manipulative. Trust and long-term commitment are not earned through communication alone. But it is one of the cornerstones of any collective achievement and one of the key skills of an effective leader.

Communication rests on two main pillars: the ability to understand and the ability to be understood. We'll take a closer look at the ability to understand in subsequent chapters, but let's focus now on a major asset: the ability to be understood.

**Question 9: what stories do I tell?**

As we all know, the best way to capture someone's attention is to tell them a good story. Children love them. So do adults. This truth has been the subject of a great deal of research and publications. We speak of storytelling or narrative communication. To put it simply, narrative communication consists in replacing an argument with a story. To combine arguments, like notes, sharps and flats, into a melodious score that awakens the senses, creates emotion, exacerbates identification with the story and facilitates memorisation.

I can tell you that I am brave and I keep my cool under all circumstances. You either believe it or you don't. You may or may not be interested. Before you know it, you'll have forgotten all about it. On the other hand, I can share the story of the armed assault I suffered many years ago in Brazil and the cold-bloodedness I displayed that undoubtedly saved my life. Well articulated, this story ticks all the boxes of good narrative communication. It generates emotion, keeps listeners on the edge of their seats and gets the message across. Some of you, running into me years later or packing your bags for Rio, will remember my experience.

In this age of social media with its staggering quantity of services or goods, its shortage of talent and its plethora of investment opportunities, it is becoming increasingly difficult to capture attention. It is therefore essential to develop the ability to tell the story of your ideas and proposals.

The fields of application are multiple. You can create an organisational narrative for investors, sponsors, customers or job applicants. You can create a team or project narrative, as you might do for employees. You can also create a personal narrative (as we did in question 1). It is also an excellent way of communicating the values of an organisation or group.

Instead of proclaiming to the world that courage and ethics are two essential values in your company, you can create a personal narrative that illustrates how they concern you. I remember a corporate exercise in which all leaders, starting at the top, were asked to prepare examples illustrating each of the company's values through personal experience. Even today, I remember the story of the vice-president, human resources in EMEA, who illustrated courage with an example: as a young HR, he had been sent to a striking mine in the middle of the Australian bush to calm tempers and negotiate a truce. I remember not only the story, but also the narrator and his attitude at that precise moment, and, more remarkably, I remember that courage was one of the company's key values, years after leaving. It's unlikely a poster would have had the same impact.

In the field of marketing, studies have shown that a product presented through the personal story of its creator or a user encourages a greater perceived value, ranging from a few percent to several tens of percent. Not to mention the impact of the story on the retention of existing customers or users. To attract, motivate and retain employees or partners, there's nothing like a good narrative. Especially when it is well integrated by everyone and not just a pretty slogan posted on a wall or on a site and recited without conviction. At the end of the day, a good narrative is something you believe in and live, not just words on paper.

Take out your reflective notebook.

- How does storytelling apply to your situation? how does that resonate?

- In what situations should you present a narrative?

- To which audience?

- In what form (written, oral, small group, large audience)?

To help you prepare your story, take one of the situations listed above: for example, explaining my career to a recruiter, presenting a new concept, engaging my management committee or convincing the board.

Think about what you're going to tell (a personal experience, a revealing event, the results of an analysis or investigation), choose the protagonist(s) (yourself, another person the audience can identify with or a group of people) Then unfold the story in the form of an adventure by answering the following questions:

- The ambition, the vision sought from the outset. It must create desire, identification and emotion.

- Obstacles on the route. What are the difficulties encountered? You have to provoke identification, empathy and curiosity.

- Show the solution found to allow the story to unfold smoothly. A product, a service, an approach, a strategy, the organisation's mission and vision.

- Conclude with lessons learned: what we've become, what we've learned, what's become clearer, what would have happened if I/we hadn't done anything.

Practise telling the story a few times, alone or with a few accomplices. Ask for their feedback. Pay attention to the three Vs:

- Verbal (your preparation, content).

- Vocal (the tone, volume and modulation of your voice).

- Visual (your appearance, attitude, non-verbal behaviour, gestures, gaze).

Even if your text is intended for the written word, do the exercise orally.

- How do you feel your narrative?

- Does it resonate with you or does it feel like a mere recitation?

Repeat the exercise, modifying it if necessary, until you feel the narrative. You're all set.

**Question 10: who do I communicate with?**

Tell me who your friends are, it's said, and I'll tell you who you are. Similarly, to achieve your objectives, you will identify the right stakeholders and develop a communication strategy with each of them that takes account of their objectives and personality, while staying focused on your goal. You'll approach each of them with a currency of exchange that they desire in return for the services, resources or time required to reach your objectives. They may provide you with information, recommendations, authorisations, financial, logistical or human resources, take on part of the work, so that you can focus on your priorities.

In this dynamic, you will debit your relationship account with each of them. You will take some of their resources, such as time, effort, money or energy, and divert them from other options. In exchange, you are going to credit those same accounts with a currency available to you and of value to them. When we say value, it can obviously mean money. But there are many other types of values. You can exchange your advice for money, your time for remuneration, for example, but also the promise of learning or a meeting.

In this exercise, emotional intelligence is paramount, depending on knowing the parties involved, their ambitions, their indicators of success, their values and, above all, their hierarchy of values, their strengths, their driving forces, their personalities. In this respect, it is important to remember that a relationship account can be credited proactively. It is always easier to debit a positive account. Relationships need to be nurtured. Life as a couple is an excellent example.

The best way to ruin your couple is to credit the account in the early years with multiple seductions, thoughtful gestures, time, listening and positive words. Once a routine has been established, you spend less and less time with your partner, tender gestures become rarer and daily reproaches fly. These regular micro-debits gradually drain the accounts with a cumulative effect and you end up in the negative, living on credit. One day, a crisis erupts, an event occurs, the straw that breaks the camel's back or the ultimate debit and bankruptcy ensues. Let's not wait until the accounts run dry before topping them up with credit.

Another way to debit the relationship account with someone is by spending time with someone else, thus giving the impression of favouritism or preference. As a leader, your visibility demands balance and fairness in exchanges. When the trust capital, or relational account, is positive with stakeholders, spending more time with one than the other is not a problem. It is the leader's right to see whomever they want and schedules will change according to the situation, although it is worth being aware of possible perceptions and interpretations.

For example, an expatriate executive was living alone in a host town, overseeing a department in a multinational company. His direct collaborators were either expatriates and single, in a couple or with a family, expatriates or locals. He spends many evenings in the bars where he meets up with some of his single colleagues. Over time, these drinking parties create a sense of complicity and closeness that creates a feeling of inequity within the department. And the alcohol makes it easier to leak unfortunate information.

Unsurprisingly, it didn't end well for the executive in question.

Another example: a highly competent team leader, who complains that her teams don't respect her authority. After discussion with each team member, it becomes clear that the team is acting with good intent. They feel that they are under-represented in the community compared to other teams. In their view, their leader doesn't spend enough time with external stakeholders, which is detrimental to them. The teams therefore took the initiative by default to raise their profile. A good realisation of the dynamics and a meeting were enough to set the record straight.

A leader of a smaller company spread over two sites in two different countries: she meets her direct reports one by one or when they get together as a group once a month, mainly to go over the figures. There is no sharing of ideas or strategic discussions. The leader spends much more time with the level below and makes no secret of it. She wants to empower them. But without realising it, she is causing confusion and mistrust at every level. Her direct reports observe her many interactions with their direct reports. They are not always informed. Contradictory orders are given. The direct reports feel disowned and those on the second tier are uncomfortable. They are reluctant to commit themselves without a signal from their line managers which irritates the leader, who sees it as a lack of initiative and courage. The result is indescribable chaos, a cascade of departures and frequent sick leave.

The chair of a major group is called in to take on the role of interim chief executive after the previous one's sudden departure. He spends most of his time face to face with his chief financial officer and blocks the rest of the management committee from the board of directors. Distrust sets in and behind-the-scenes manoeuvring multiplies. In the meantime, the group's financial situation is at an all-time low. While the situation calls for the management committee to unite around the relaunch project, considerable energy is lost in political games and sterile speculation.

These four situations are all specific, but they have one thing in common: the impact of unbalanced or inequitable, poorly controlled relationships on stakeholders, leading to the perception, whether justified or not, it doesn't matter, of a form of inequity. To a certain extent, these imbalances are inevitable. However, as a leader, we need to remain vigilant to avoid unnecessarily debiting the relational accounts with people who are useful to the achievement of our long-term objectives.

In your notebook, take one of your key objectives or ambitions.

- List the key stakeholders needed to make them happen, such as employees, colleagues, managers, authorities, interest groups, the press or mentors.

- Name them individually or group them by category if there are too many. Be aware, however, that the greater their number, the more difficult it is to actively manage our network.

- Assign a score to the quality of the trust capital (relationship account) with each of these people or categories from one to five. Take their perspective.

- If I asked them to describe the quality of their relationship with you, what would they say?

- Evaluate each of their currencies and whether you're prepared to pay them. Now take a step back. What can you see?

- Is your network adequate and fair?

- Do you see any trust deficits and obstacles to good interaction? How do you plan to deal with them?

- How do you intend to manage your stakeholders effectively?

**Question 11: how do I communicate?**

When it comes to communication, trust is everything. Whether you know your contacts well or not at all, the chances of getting their attention and contribution will depend first and foremost on how much trust you have. To assess it, I like the trust equation developed by David Maister, a former Harvard Business School professor, which relies on four factors, three of which are in the numerator.

- **Your credibility**: this is determined by your achievements, your track record, your results, your reputation. People can estimate your credibility on the basis of their own experience, hearsay or external signs (your address, appearance, dress, diplomas etc).

- **Your reliability**: based on people's experience or your reputation. If your contact knows that they can ask you for something with their eyes closed and that you always deliver on time, they will give you a high mark on the reliability factor. Of course, trust and reliability go hand in hand. In the long run, it is hard to maintain credibility if you're unreliable. Conversely, rock-solid reliability can help build credibility. But at any given moment, the two do not necessarily coincide.

- **Intimacy**: or the degree of closeness. How well does the other person know me? Do they feel comfortable with me?

The higher the score on these three factors, the greater the level of trust; each can be evaluated on a scale of one to three, for example, and added together.

The denominator is the perceived level of egocentricity or self-orientation: does my contact perceive me as driven by our mutual interest? or rather by my own exclusive (egocentric) interest? The higher the perceived egocentricity, the higher the score, the greater the negative impact on trust.

Choose a contact who is essential to achieving your objectives. Adopt their perspective. How would they rate you from one (low) to three (high)? The ideal for confidence is three for each factor in the numerator, giving a total of nine, and one in the denominator for a total of nine points. Worst case, three in the numerator and three in the denominator for a total of one point.

It is also a good idea to assess how much you trust this person. As part of a team dynamic, I sometimes organise face-to-face exchanges where each member shares their scores with the others. It's a useful way to reinforce the intimacy factor. It is not an exercise for everyone, however, and should only be proposed if the conditions of honesty, trust and openness are met. You can also have an open discussion using the trust equation to structure it. I sometimes use it with colleagues to seek for and provide feedback.

At the end of the day, this capital of trust will undeniably condition the impact of your communication. Poorly mastered communication will do less damage to its author, and will be more easily forgiven, if they have high trust capital from the outset.

Whatever the case, mastering communication is an essential asset for leaders. Start with your priority objectives and ambitions; know your stakeholders and the currencies that matter to them; and, once you've assessed the trust capital you possess, there's nothing left to do but prepare your communication.

Choosing the right channel is crucial. Are we going to communicate orally or in writing, face to face or virtually, in a large group or one by one? Context and timing are also important. Are you the right person to get this message across to these people? Is the timing right?

One thing's for sure: the more emotion generated, the more attention and retention. Generating the right emotion is essential. People always remember more about how they felt when they met you than what you told them. If they remember something you said, it is not because of the word itself, but because of the emotion it generated.

When it comes to learning, we learn best when we experience learning with emotion. That's why we learn more by doing things ourselves in the field or in a simulation than by passively following a course and why we prefer a good discussion to a lecture. That's why we learn more from a narrative and why we're more likely to influence our contacts if we can trigger emotions like joy, pride, shame, guilt or sadness.

Effective communication, whatever the context, audience size and channel chosen, will have more impact if we consider the following elements, the five key criteria for impactful communication.

- **Audience**: getting to know your audience (whether a single person or a group). What is their objective or ambition? What currency are they sensitive to? What emotion will I activate? If the news I bring is bad, how will my audience want to hear it?

- **Objective**: be clear about your goal. What is my long-term objective? What is my concrete objective at the end of this specific communication? Try to visualise as clearly as possible what your audience will do or say at the end of your intervention?

  A few years ago, I remember a manager who wanted to speak at one of my meetings.

  'Olivier, can you give me a 20-minute slot?'

  'No problem. What for?'

  'Well, I'd like to tell them about our project.'

  'Okay, but why?

  'Well, to let them know.'

  'Yes, and then what do you want them to do with it?'

  'What do you mean?'

  By asking the question why three times, once I'd got past the director's astonishment and even annoyance, I helped him to clarify his real, concrete intention. Do I want to present a project so that the teams can talk about it, tick a box or ask them to do something specific? And if so, what exactly? The clearer and more precise it is in our heads, the more likely we are to create impactful communication.

- **Key points**: identify a few key points, ideally around three, and build your communication around them. They can include: a chronological sequence (before, during, after); key arguments or benefits (easy to use, inexpensive, delivered quickly); or independent points (molecule 1, delivery times, points to consider).

Each key point can be developed in detail in a tree structure. Without losing sight of the original framework. This three-point structure is a good way of forcing ourselves to remain concise and to emphasise the essentials without overlooking the details, thanks to the development of a tree structure. It offers the best chance of maximising the impact of our communication by playing on the two retention mechanisms: retention by sensing and retention by intuition. Each of us has their own preferred mode of retention. In the first case, the brain prints sequences and factual elements lined up one after the other. In the second, it conceives an overall vision, identifies links between different points and then, if necessary, looks for detailed elements to support the whole. Depending on the person and the circumstances, one means will be preferred to the other, and by using the technique of key points and tree structures, you maximise the chances of communicating effectively to both types of audience.

- **Recap**: conclude your message by summarising the key points. To increase the chances of retention and provide maximum clarity.

- **Incentive**: end with a reminder of what specifically you expect from your audience. What do I suggest you do at the end of this communication?

Now take a situation that requires communication on your part: are you the right person to communicate that message?

(think of the trust equation: credibility, reliability, intimacy and egocentricity). If so, what communication channel do you think is appropriate in the circumstances? Prepare your communication using the five key criteria listed below:

- Audience / ambition / outcome

- Your ambitions / long-term goal  after your communication

- Key points / framework and tree structure

- Recap

- Incentives / your expectations / your proposals

**Conclusion**

Communication is one of the pillars of any human society. It is the glue that binds each individual to the others and to the whole, whether family, association, organisation or society at large. Often, lack of communication or poor communication is considered one of the most common dysfunctions among leaders. Yet communication is often taken for granted, as it has been part of our lives since birth. Most of us learn to communicate by trial and error.

In the best cases, we become aware of the feedback our communication provokes and adjust as experience dictates. In the worst cases, we blame others without realising that we're participating in the loop of misunderstanding. Just like the commuter who rages against the traffic they are stuck in, wondering what all those people are doing on the roads when they get behind the wheel. Communication is so ingrained in our DNA that, in its absence, we fill in the blanks, imagine and interpret. Silence speaks as much as words.

And every gesture, every word spread in one corner of the world has a butterfly effect thousands of kilometres away, amplified by human and technological relays. In this respect, technology is a good thing. Let's not forget that behind every smartphone, behind every screen, there's a human being.

Human beings are both the purpose and the vehicle of communication. The major obstacle to good communication and a more harmonious collective life lies in human diversity itself. We are each a combination of temperaments, unique experiences, backgrounds, beliefs, values, social and educational backgrounds, cultures, trans-generational histories and multiple sensitivities which, combined, represent a unique whole that sets us apart from all our contemporaries.

So, it is only logical that, faced with a given situation, no two people will see and feel things in exactly the same way. Just look at the difficulty we sometimes have in understanding our spouse, our parents or our children. Despite all the love we have for them.

Then imagine the chances of understanding and communicating well with colleagues, customers, co-workers or any other people where the initial benevolence is not necessarily present. What's the point in trying to improve? Yet effective communication is the key to collective and individual success, calling on us to decode our current and future contacts, and to consider our communication with them in a strategic and controlled way, while retaining our authenticity. A wonderful paradox. Another one. Leadership is all about reconciling paradoxes.

# 4

# LACK OF VISION

*'A vision without action is just a dream. Action that doesn't follow vision is time wasted. A vision followed by action can change the world.'*

**Nelson Mandela,
South African statesman**

*'When you have a clear vision of your goal, it is easier to take the first step towards making it a reality.'*

**Japanese proverb**

# LACK OF VISION

**The challenge**: inspire and guide action and change by providing an engaging, collective perspective.

**The risk**: scare away talent, engender apathy or neglect, come across as a mere controller, provoke the formation of silos, exacerbate resistance to change.

**The opportunity**: rally people around a cause, a vision or a project through an engaging approach and communication. Inspire. Convince. Create trust. Clarify. Get results.

**The response**: three questions to strengthen your sense of vision.

- What perspectives would I like to exploit and share?

- What energy do I project around me?

- How can I facilitate change and agility?

## Creating emotional bonds for change

A passing tourist observes a man carrying a stone with great difficulty, looking downcast and sad. 'What are you doing without being nosey?', he asks.

'I am carrying a stone', replies the man with a haggard look.

A little further on, another man is also carrying a stone. He looks more dynamic than the first. The tourist approaches him and asks, 'why are you carrying that stone?'.

'Well, it is my job. I can feed my family', replies the man.

Curious, the tourist spots a third man. He moves briskly, a stone in his hands, humming. 'Is this your job? What exactly do you do?'

'Yes, I am a builder and I am building the biggest cathedral in the world,' replies the man, pride in his eyes.

This story illustrates just how much the goal we're pursuing, and our emotional connection to it, can make a difference when it comes to enthusiasm, motivation and perseverance. There are three types of motivation.

I can clean the room because I love cleaning and, when I am cleaning, I forget about the passage of time. This is an intrinsic type of motivation, often the most powerful, which brings pleasure and meaning. It is what drives our third man, the cathedral builder.

I can clean the room because, without being passionate about the activity, I anticipate a result. This is the case of our second man, who expects to be paid in exchange for his work but puts his heart into it despite everything. This is extrinsic motivation.

Or I can clean the room because, even if I don't like the activity, and, even if I don't quite understand what it is for, I feel I must do it. This is the lowest level of motivation, amotivation. Amotivated people engage in an activity without really knowing why they're doing it and without really knowing what they're getting out of it. This is the case with our first man.

There's no value judgement on my part regarding the motivations of any of them. It turns out that the combination of intrinsic and extrinsic motivations is often used to set humans in motion. However, intrinsic motivation offers the best return on investment, releasing the most energy with the least fuel.

Think of the concessions that many young (and not so young) talents are prepared to make for the chance to work for a high-profile company that is revolutionising our lives and bringing meaning to the job. Compare it to the financial efforts (extrinsic motivations) that other, less hyped companies have to make to remain competitive on the job market. That's why it is so important to give meaning to our projects, communicate clearly about them and offer an engaging perspective.

## Question 12: what perspectives would I like to exploit and share?

Visionary leaders have a profound and lasting impact on their environment. They generally possess the following qualities: they challenge the status quo and reinvent codes, they anticipate and look to the future, they have their feet on the ground, they have the patience to transform their environment in pursuit of their vision, they are willing to step out of their comfort zone and they have exceptional mental agility.

We often think of visionary leaders at the top of organisations but two things are clear. Firstly, the leader at the top of an organisation is not automatically a visionary. Some leaders have reached the top because they have superb transactional skills and wield spreadsheets, carrots and sticks brilliantly. Which, let's face it, is often a valuable asset, but not necessarily sufficient.

Secondly, there are visionary leaders at all levels of organisations who have a ripple effect on their teams and those around them. In this respect, I recall a European multinational with a regional office in Sydney. I was invited to work with a group of leaders from this part of the world on their leadership. The programme was residential, two hours' drive from Sydney, in a part of the world where the number of skin clinics exceeds the number of nursery schools, and where golf courses are overrun not by rabbits in the early morning but by kangaroos.

Many of the leaders shared their frustrations with me. The parent company was a big, report-hungry bureaucracy, and their room for manoeuvre was limited. One evening, part of the group of Indian origin wanted to leave the hotel for dinner at an Indian restaurant in the neighbouring town. They asked me to accompany them. I accepted enthusiastically. We were going to swap meat pies and Tooheys for curries and Cobras.

The conversation quickly turned to their company and their jobs. Curious to know more about the restrictions imposed by head office, I decided to broach the subject. The reaction of one of the leaders was a real eye-opener: 'oh no, Olivier, we have a great deal of autonomy in this group. We've got great products, a well-known brand, and when we have an idea, we can test it and implement it. When things don't go our way, we find a way to make it happen anyway'.

At this point, all the smiling heads nodded from left to right as one. Eye opening, because all these leaders were working together, they had the same means and the same constraints. Yet this sub-group's version was different from what I had heard earlier from their more voluble colleagues.

A year later, by chance, I met one of the group's European managers, who had worked in the region. I shared this anecdote with him, concluding: 'their mindset was so different, positive and enthusiastic, focused on vision, that it wouldn't surprise me if in five to ten years' time, they occupied all the key positions'. To which my contact replied: 'five to ten years? That's already the case. In fact, it is causing quite a stir among others, who are crying discrimination'.

Regardless of the characteristics of any particular sub-group, this story demonstrates the natural ripple effect that an enthusiastic person connected to a vision can have on those around them. In short, cathedral builders have more positive influence and leadership than stone carriers.

Visionary leaders focus relentlessly on what they need to achieve and overcome any constraints that stand in their way. They present a long-term direction and context, obtaining the support and commitment of those around them. Their role is to share information and create a space for ongoing dialogue. They offer a broad perspective and help their teams define how to get there. It is not just about presenting a vision on special occasions or at a meeting. It is about regularly defining the context (why, what, what's in it for me?) that team members need to stay focused, engaged and performing at their best.

Take out your reflective notebook. As a leader, you must wear many hats depending on the circumstances. You need to lead, set the tone, empower, coach, empathise and inspire. As a visionary leader, you provide a long-term perspective and help your teams, through ongoing dialogue, to take ownership of the responsibilities required to achieve results.

- How would you assess your role as a visionary leader?

- How do you set aside time and mental space to observe, listen, establish a dialogue beyond your transactional responsibilities to anticipate transformations and trends?

- What is your outlook in the medium and long term?

- What new avenues are opening up for you?

- How do you mobilise the people around you?

- What should you change?

- Who should you mobilise more?

- What are the opportunities and risks?

- How can you help your teams move out of their comfort zone and become more agile?

**Question 13: what energy do I project around me?**

Charisma, from the Greek *khárisma*, the gift of divine grace, has been the subject of much discussion and debate. Visionary leaders are often associated with charisma, although it is far from unanimous. So perhaps we should take a closer look at what we mean by charisma.

Among the conflicting things we read are 'an authority, a natural ascendancy provoking a strong adhesion in other people', 'the visionary who wins the hearts of crowds by inspiring and inciting others to believe in their vision', 'something you're born with', 'who has presence, who seduces, influences others thanks to their speech and their way of expressing themselves', 'belief in the powers of charismatic leaders is overestimated when we look at their real effect on business performance', 'charismatic leaders have caused serious damage to society' and 'charismatic leaders sometimes engage in self-promotion, but the image they want to project sometimes turns out to be very different from reality'. So, who and what to believe?

First, the aura we associate with charisma is made up of an energy, a halo that impresses, attracts, dazzles and even fascinates. It helps to attract others. So, a priori, it is useful if you want to assert your leadership. Secondly, charisma is associated with the ability to easily express your thoughts. Public speaking is closely linked to charisma. Charisma also emanates from poise, from a controlled attitude, from a presence conferred by the assurance of your convictions and by the ability to present things with conviction, clarity and quiet strength. Of course, the strength of conviction is not always proportional to the benefit it generates. After all, charisma is likely to dull the vigilance and critical faculties of the audience; it does not necessarily guarantee the sincere generosity of its bearer. Charisma is not automatically synonymous with a win-win situation.

Secondly, we often associate it with something innate, a gift we're born with. Yet charisma can appear later in life. The charisma of some great leaders emerged as they developed a strong conviction and as they found a sympathetic audience with whom to share it. So, while certain innate predispositions can facilitate the development of charisma, it is closely linked to a firm conviction, developed over time, that gives a strong assurance, a depth, that will radiate, give off an aura, an overflowing energy. So, innate or acquired? Probably both. A gift from god? When it comes to charisma, we can certainly apply the adage, 'help yourself and heaven will help you'.

Many years ago, I had the opportunity to work with two charismatic leaders, both Americans, who were members of the management committee in a US multinational. The first was flamboyant, Californian, charming, with a moon-beam smile. He was adored. The second from a minority, born in a small town in the Deep South, was introverted. Her charisma was chilling. A phone call from her at dawn acted like a defibrillator shot on the sleepiest.

One spoke loudly and quickly, his face was full of life, his gestures free and flowing. The other expressed herself slowly with a deep voice, sparing gestures and frozen facial muscles. Nevertheless, what they both had in common was a strong conviction in their respective fields, an ability to articulate their ideas, and a radiant presence and attitude. Each was charismatic in their own way. So, you can be charismatic with different styles. You can also be charismatic for some people and not for others. The perception of charisma probably varies from one group to another, from one culture to another.

I once saw a Japanese speaker whose volume and rhythm of voice would have instantly put the average Westerner into a deep sleep. He had the same effect on me as an audio book you listen to at 11 pm, before going to sleep (or, more accurately, with the aim of falling asleep). Yet it seemed to hold its audience in suspense. You could feel the depth of the subject matter.

One day in Shanghai, at the end of a conference, a Chinese participant came up to me to thank and congratulate me, adding that he had only one comment to make: I had a Hollywood style. I'd heard many adjectives used to describe my communication style, but I must admit that this was the first time, and the last, that anyone used the term to describe me. I am not sure Californians would feel the same way.

Let's not forget that when it comes to communication and aura, we can draw a parallel with water: the same amount of water can drown the cactus and dry out the bamboo. Aura and charisma can therefore take on different forms from one audience to another. Without exception, however, the charismatic leader's energy emanates from a healthy body. I've often found that charismatic people have a healthy, disciplined lifestyle that enables them to manage their energy capital and maintain their soul and body. It could even be said that charisma is the visible part of self-esteem.

- Are the prospects you see for the future based on deep-seated convictions? if so, which ones?

- Are they just a matter of circumstance or have they been with you for a long time?

- Are your convictions ethical and defensible?

- What's your level of empathy? how does it help strengthen your aura?

- How would you rate your ability to articulate your convictions clearly and confidently?

- What does your attitude, posture and body language convey?

- Do they help you showcase your convictions?

- What are your innate strengths and what can you do to work on your charisma?

- What do you do to maintain your energy?

**Question 14: how can I facilitate change and agility?**

When I found myself in a hospital bed for several weeks, and then convalescing for several months, one of the major discoveries I made was that recovering mental energy is much slower and more arduous than recovering physical energy. I found it much easier to get back into sport than into work. Thinking wasn't really a problem. What was really difficult was to take a position, to decide, to assemble all the elements of a reflection and draw a conclusion. I wanted simplicity, I wanted a manual job, and I am not a manual person at all.

For the first time, I felt physically how much mental energy is required to think and decide. I was trying to think of different scenarios for getting out of the post-Covid crisis, and I would immediately close my eyes to go back to sleep. I deeply, physically felt the temptation to let things take their course and rely on others to do things and think for me. This was a real breakthrough insofar as, despite knowing that you need energy to live and move forward, experiencing it myself really helped me realise one thing: most people intuitively know what they need to do to improve their situation, but the main obstacle to change is often the lack of energy required to make choices and set in motion the necessary habit changes. So, by default, they procrastinate and carry on doing things as before on autopilot.

This procrastination is not necessarily a sign of laziness or ignorance, but a way of escaping the discomfort of decision-making and change. Because, however open we are to change, as human beings, we're designed to cling to certainty and stability. The only way to transcend this malaise is to find a sufficiently compelling reason to change, a sufficiently pressing why, and to define clear and reassuring milestones, small steps to reach the goal. This is what I did to get out of my convalescence and get back to exciting projects, such as writing this book.

I took enough time to reflect on my real motivation for writing it, the why. I anticipated the eventuality of dying without having written it, until the image was unbearable, and then I decided to take the first step, by writing a first chapter, just to see, and then a second, and then a third, and then I told myself that I'd written quite a few pages and that I couldn't decently leave this document to rot on a server. I realised that I could write. I was doomed to continue. Then, little by little, I got into the habit of writing. I also sought out accomplices, who each in their own way acted as coaches.

This brings me to the role of a leader in the change process. Leaders face the same natural resistance to change. Like all human beings, they aspire to avoid unnecessary disruption. However, they differ from the majority in several respects.

- They anticipate more than the others and see a reason to change before they do.

- They find a why and make it compelling to the point where the prospect of the status quo becomes unpleasant, even intolerable.

- They find the energy to take the first tiny step and put in place a plan of action and routines that will give them the boost and discipline every morning.

- They build bridges to their stakeholders and put in place a communication strategy and a framework of action, support and follow-up to help them find their why, then get them to take their first small steps, make the quick wins, and involve them in the process of defining and executing change.

These steps apply to any situation, whether you want to change career, location, lifestyle or implement a new programme within your organisation. Change management models all revolve around these points and focus on three main areas:

- Drive change by creating a sense of urgency (reinforcing the perceived why and passing on the sense of urgency to others), surrounding yourself with a team of trailblazers and developing a strategic vision with them.

- Achieve change by communicating, involving teams and reassuring them with tangible intermediate results as soon as possible (the small steps).

- Consolidate by communicating successes and embedding new behaviours and processes in habits and culture.

Now reflect and ask yourself:

- Generally speaking, what are your natural, personal resistances to change?

- What are your unique personal assets?

- On a more specific level, what are the changes you need to make right now?

- Faced with these necessary changes that you anticipate, what are you doing to create a favourable personal dynamic?

- Are you firmly convinced of the need to change?

- Are you sure that change is preferable to the status quo?

- If so, what steps need to be defined to achieve this?

- What new routines do you personally need to establish? what could get in the way?

- How do you deal with this?

- How are you going to measure the small steps and celebrate the first wins?

- Who can act as your mentor, coach, sparring partner or sounding board?

- On a collective level, considering the need to drive, implement and consolidate change, what have you put in place?

- What's left to do?

- What is becoming clearer to you about your role in the change?

**Conclusion**

Every human action is the result of a vision. That's undeniable. The real question is: whose vision?

Every morning, billions of men and women get up to fulfil someone else's vision: to go to school, to the army, to work in a company, a hospital or in the civil service. Of course, there may be something in it for them. But fulfilment and accomplishment are rooted in a personal vision that finds an outlet for expression. This personal vision may be part of a broader, more collective vision.

A leader's vision can be either personal or one that they embrace according to their aspirations or struggles. They draw into their wake men and women who recognise themselves in their vision, who believe in their ability to implement it, and who benefit from it, at least temporarily, or ideally over the long term. Lack of vision, or failure to communicate the vision, is often cited as one of the key criticisms of leaders.

# 5

# DISPERSION

*'The man who chases two hares catches neither.'*

**Confucius, Chinese philosopher**

*'The victorious warrior is an ordinary man with laser-like concentration.'*

**Bruce Lee, icon of martial arts cinema**

# DISPERSION

**The challenge**: optimise the deployment of available resources, channel energies and avoid unnecessary wastage.

**The risk**: not making a clear-cut decision, wanting to embrace everything at once, becoming exhausted, creating confusion, wasting resources.

**The opportunity**: align and organise resources optimally. Make courageous choices and prioritise. Creating order in chaos. Manage conflicts in time.

**The response**: focus with two questions.

- How can I contribute to the alignment, optimisation and focus of the resources available?

- What role can I play in anticipating and managing conflicts?

## Choosing means giving up

A company once decided to expand its product range to seize the market's potential and take the competition by storm. The sales team was delighted. They had plenty of room to manoeuvre and could respond to any customer request. If necessary, they even took the initiative of offering specific customisations, in the form of samples, to convince even the most reluctant prospects. As you may have guessed, it didn't necessarily make production any happier.

The exponential multiplication of stock-keeping units demanded constant changes to the schedule. Constant changes to parameter settings led to costly interruptions to production and late deliveries to major customers. Not to mention the breakdowns. The new machines were designed for high volumes purchased with a view to ramping up production and optimising costs. They were not designed for short runs of samples.

Production took their grievances to the top of the organisation. Sales did the same, feeling that production was not customer-oriented enough and was getting in their way. The issue was put on the agenda for a board meeting. In the end, it was decided that sales had to be more proactive in their forecasts and that production had to be more flexible. In other words, nothing was really decided.

A new weekly meeting was set up between production, planning and sales. But as you might expect, nothing really changed. Delays and breakdowns accumulated, as did frustrations. Production costs continued to rise. The chief executive called a meeting with the supply chain director, sales director and production manager. After several heated discussions, all agreed to reduce SKUs by 30 percent and optimise the catalogue.

Product management was asked to propose a new catalogue and analyse each existing part number in order to make optimisation choices. The sales director was invited to participate actively in the exercise and to align his sales teams. The decision was made. Soon after, the sales director left the company for personal reasons. He was replaced by a new manager who, after analysis, proposed to launch three new test markets to accelerate growth.

Production got upset and did not understand the chief executive's logic or at least the timing. From experience, they knew that entering new markets meant producing numerous small series and new references to stand out from the competition, attract new customers and win their loyalty. This ran counter to the decision to reduce part numbers, breakdowns and costs.

Faithful to the decision to reduce part numbers by 30 percent, production logically refused a request from sales to provide a non-standard sample for a potential customer in one of the new markets. The sales manager raised the issue and the chief executive was called in to arbitrate, who decided that the customer was the priority and forced production to meet the request.

As you can see, it is a case of the cat biting the tail. The best team building wouldn't help: it wasn't the teams that didn't get along and it wasn't the employees who lacked initiative. In fact, the level of understanding and initiative was remarkable, given the prevailing chaos.

The problem was the lack of arbitration by the general manager. Seen like that, it is pretty obvious. When you look at things from a distance, you understand quickly. On the other hand, when you're in the situation, it is harder for the protagonists to spot. Everyone has good reasons for not changing. And the solution isn't easy. Because to choose, to decide, means to give up, and every option implies renunciations and risks. Not choosing means wasting time, chaos and energy.

**Question 15: how can I contribute to the alignment, optimisation and focus of the resources available?**

Today, agility and creativity are the order of the day in many organisations. Confronted on the one hand with new generations who are more demanding in terms of autonomy in a tense job market, where talent is coveted and therefore in a position of strength, and on the other hand with increasingly pampered customers in search of innovation, leaders need to promote creativity and autonomy. This context has seen the emergence of new, more collective and democratic modes of organisation and decision-making.

These models work well in phases of divergence. All teams are involved in the upstream process of proposal and idea generation. Collective intelligence is solicited and developed. Responsibilities are shared. However, there comes a time when we have to move from divergent to convergent mode. Decisions and choices have to be made. They may emanate from the collective. Or they may fall to a decision-maker.

In the more collective approach, consensus is possible. However, this requires a high level of mutual trust, a strong sense of the common good and the availability of time. Sometimes one or more of these elements is lacking. When things drag on, someone has to make a decision, which will automatically displease some people and provoke criticism.

I once worked with a non-governmental organisation where the values of equality and consensus were so deeply entrenched that the people involved found it difficult to reach a decision on key issues for the future of the organisation. The NGO decided to recruit an external director with experience in the private sector, who had to be sensitive to the NGO's cause, have financial skills and managerial experience, as well as knowing how to make decisions and arbitrate tactfully. They found the rare pearl, a director who matched the profile perfectly. So, they hired her and it wasn't long before everyone was unanimously against her. The culture of consensus was so strong that it was impossible to get anyone to accept an authoritative choice, even for the good of the organisation. Decision-making is certainly a difficult art.

It necessarily involves three stages: before, during and after. The first stage is exploration. This means taking the time to understand, listen, ask questions, observe, analyse and consult. The aim is to increase the chances of making a better decision and to involve stakeholders upstream.

The second stage is the decision. Either you can make the decision yourself. Or the decision is brought up or down to the appropriate level. Upwards, in the form of suggestions or recommendations, or downwards, in the form of total delegation. Regarding this second stage, there's a saying that goes: to make a good decision, it is better not to be more than two and preferably an odd number. As we have seen, some people prove the adage wrong and manage to make collective decisions, but without an alternative mechanism to deal with protracted disagreements, the risk of paralysis is not negligible.

The third stage is implementation. Teams are involved in implementation and consulted, drawing on their expertise, depending on their degree of maturity to define the how. At this stage, the dysfunction we're concerned with, dispersion, can take on a particular form. A single question can confuse, frustrate and undermine the leader. The question to avoid at all costs is: 'what do you think?'. While this question is perfectly appropriate in phase 1 (exploration), in phase 3 it will reopen the debate on the relevance of the decision. What we're interested in now is not what people think, but how we're going to implement it. By asking this question at the wrong time, there are only two possible outcomes:

- Either the leader is forced to close the discussion after a while, in which case they have raised false hopes in those opposed to the decision, distracted everyone from the objective by wasting their time and dispersing energies, and, in the end, everyone feels manipulated.

- Or they actively engage in the discussion. In so doing, they acknowledge de facto that the decision taken may not have been the right one. Or, at any rate, they doubt or fear the reaction of their teams, giving the impression of recognising that they didn't listen enough in phase 1. In the end, they expose to everyone their difficulty in deciding and sticking to the decision taken. Or, if they did not initiate the decision, they disassociate themselves from it.

In $360^0$ evaluations, on the subject of decision-making and team involvement, apart from certain extreme cases (excessively directive or excessively participative) there are always people who, in their feedback, consider that the leader consults adequately before making a decision and others who think the opposite. It is inevitable. Generally speaking, the person who makes suggestions and sees them incorporated into the decision will have a rather positive opinion. If the decision takes a different direction from what they had suggested, they will be more critical of the leader.

This is why a $360^0$ exercise is extremely useful as a basis for reflection, but it must be analysed with a certain amount of hindsight, particularly with regard to the leader's ability to make decisions and align their teams. Ask questions to prepare your decision-making and you'll always have people who think you don't ask enough and that you do what you want anyway. Others who will think you consult too much and should be more directive. Everyone has their own perception of the right balance and their own personal experiences in each case.

Decision-making and arbitration are rarely popular. The leader must have humility, wisdom and patience to create spaces and moments for divergence, and the foresight and courage to decide when to invite convergence, end the discussion and make the decision or have someone decide.

For a long time, it was assumed that decision-making was a purely rational process based in the prefrontal cortex associated with so-called higher functions, such as language, reasoning and, more generally, executive functions. However, more recent research shows that emotions are indispensable for reasoning and that the absence of emotional perception, after a head injury for example, can render a person irrational, while their reasoning abilities remain unaffected.

Reasoning abilities are supported by various emotional cues. If a decision is perceived by the emotion as harmful, it is automatically associated with an unpleasant sensation in the body and then rejected. If, on the other hand, the emotion felt is positive, the option is identified and retained. The energy required to make a decision, at the ultimate moment of choice and its announcement, and the courage needed to close the doors to other options are therefore associated with emotions.

We may be rational and objective during the thought process, but we're still human at the moment of decision, and in the grip of our own emotions linked to our values, fears and beliefs. Emotions of fear, shame, sadness, pride, joy, regret and remorse are activated at the moment of the ultimate choice. To ignore them is to risk becoming irrational and underestimating the impact of your decision on others.

Think of a leader pushed to the limit, who in despair, in the grip of a flood of repressed contradictory emotions, makes completely irrational decisions. Giving too much room to these emotions risks paralysis and the inability to make unpopular but necessary decisions. Ignoring or silencing them is the best way to make an irrational, and therefore inappropriate, decision.

Now think about your own current cycles of divergence and convergence:

- Where are your key projects today and where is your organisation as a whole?

- What are sensitive points that become clearer to you after reflection?

- When it comes to convergence, what opportunities do you need to focus on?

- How can you optimise the alignment and collaboration of the stakeholders involved?

- If you feel a personal reluctance to make decisions where necessary, to what do you attribute it?

- What emotions do you feel (fear, shame, sadness, pride, joy, regret, remorse)? why?

- What are your personal values at stake?

- What can you do to help your stakeholders accept the decision and take full responsibility?

- What about the sequencing of your decisions?

- Are you sure you're not initiating too many projects at once?

- What, if anything, can you do to restore the balance?

**Question 16: what role can I play in anticipating and managing conflicts?**

A major source of dispersion and wasted energy is conflict. To a certain extent, a difference of opinion or interest can be a source of opportunity. These differences do not in themselves constitute conflict. More often than not, they are the sign of a healthy environment. They provide an opportunity for open and transparent exchange and dialogue, and are the driving force behind collaboration, dialogue and creativity.

Conflict arises when the process of exchange breaks down, mistrust sets in and uncontrolled emotion stands in the way of dialogue. As a result, disagreement becomes violent and the dynamic can quickly spiral out of control. It then becomes difficult to get out of the situation. That's why it is important to anticipate conflict or, failing that, to resolve it as early as possible.

Conflict can also arise when there is an incompatibility of moods or values. In this case, the source is deeper and the resolution more complex. Whatever the case, the leader has a dual responsibility in this area. They must manage their own personal conflicts, as well as conflicts between third parties. When it comes to conflict, there are several situations with which a leader can be confronted.

- **The absence of conflict**: by definition, an ideal situation. The challenge in this case is to keep an eye on the situation and ensure that the conditions for good understanding, transparency and satisfactory collaboration are maintained. To preserve this harmony, the leader will identify, recognise and encourage behaviours that contribute to it, while remaining vigilant that the apparent calm does not conceal a smouldering fire. Or is not the result of apathy depriving the collective of an opportunity to stimulate discussions.

- **Avoidance**: in this case, a potential source of conflict exists, but the parties involved avoid talking about it, which can be advantageous. Firstly, the source of frustration and potential conflict may disappear on its own. It is better to be patient than to debit a person's relationship account by confronting them prematurely. Then, in some cases, someone else may take over the problem. Sometimes it is better to wait a while. It is not always appropriate to feel responsible, even if it seems counterintuitive for a leader. In fact, an excessive sense of responsibility is a drift that can impair a leader's effectiveness. On the other hand, avoidance can also be a risky or irresponsible attitude. Sometimes it is necessary to confront a situation before it degenerates. To prevent the conflict from escalating, or to avoid being seen as soft, cowardly or negligent.

- **The position of strength**: a latent conflict exists but remains contained because a balance of power has been established. The basis for this may be precarious or unjust, but sometimes a bad peace is better than a good war. Here too, we need to take the pulse of the situation on a regular basis, to reassess the foundations of the balance and anticipate possible shifts. If you're in a position of strength, it is worth enlisting the support of your allies to prevent any rebellion without debiting a relational account unnecessarily or creating resentment.

- **Negotiation**: in this case, the parties involved are aware of a problem, accept the premise that they are part of it, and tackle it head-on by establishing a constructive dialogue to find a solution or iron out differences. The outcome can be more or less creative. In some cases, you'll settle for a compromise where everyone puts water in their wine. When there's time and a minimum of trust between the parties, you'll try to find a third, more creative way to create additional value for all parties.

- **Mediation**: when negotiation fails, or when the parties are unwilling or unable to engage in it, or when avoidance is neither possible nor desirable, or when the balance of power shifts, the parties involved can agree to call on a third party perceived as neutral, whose role is to assist in dialogue and decision-making. It is a supporting role played by a person who enjoys a certain moral legitimacy in the eyes of both parties. The leader may be involved.

- **Arbitration**: when all else fails, arbitration remains the solution. An accepted, legitimate or imposed authority, a third party perceived as neutral, is invited to facilitate dialogue and make the final decision.

Think of a conflict, whether actual or latent, that concerns you.

- Is the status quo possible and desirable?

- If not, are you ready to play a more active role?

- What would you like to change?

- What would be the most favourable outcome? the minimum acceptable? a reasonable middle ground?

- What would be your personal goal in making this change?

- What's in it for the parties involved?

- What should your strategy be?

- Impose? slice and dice?

- Provoke discussion and follow the change proposed by others?

- Tactically avoid for now?

- Negotiate?

- Coaching and facilitating mediated negotiations?

- Arbitration?

**Conclusion**

The leader has an essential responsibility: to rally and engage stakeholders in order to achieve a mission and reach objectives. They must optimise the resources available, relying on various stakeholders for support and commitment, while ensuring they work in concert.

In an exercise I sometimes propose to my clients in the Swiss mountains, participants must lead a flock of sheep back into a pen. First, the dogs show them how it is done and then the leaders take over. This exercise is revealing. If you stand too close to the sheep, they panic, get upset and freeze. If you stand too far away, they go off in all directions. Striking the right balance is an art that the leader must master.

To use another metaphor, they are like a practitioner of *capoeira,* the dancelike martial art from Brazil. Between the two performers, one represents the leader, the other the stakeholder. As a  martial art, it is not about striking, but about supple, acrobatic movements. There's an ambivalence in this art, since it is a fight, but no blows are landed, and the art is also like a playful, acrobatic dance.

Sometimes the leader has to take the helm firmly and bring along people who are not always 100 percent aligned or whose personal interests may diverge somewhat from the objectives of the leader or the organisation they represent. This is essential to avoid dispersion. But they must avoid throwing punches and, like a *capoeira* practitioner, ensure that exchanges remain fluid and value-bearing for all parties, in order to move the whole forward and achieve the common goal in a positive climate.

# 6

## MISTRUST

*'Confidence is like blood pressure. It doesn't make a sound, it is vital to health and, if neglected, can prove fatal.'*

Frank Sonnenberg, US author

*'Trust is a greater compliment than love.'*

George MacDonald, Scottish
author, poet and minister

# MISTRUST

**The challenge**: create a climate of trust to encourage the assumption of responsibility and the development of collective intelligence.

**The risk**: create psychological insecurity, discourage initiative-taking and deprive yourself of adequate, honest and timely feedback.

**The opportunity**: encourage autonomy and risk-taking. Promote innovation. Create an agile, inclusive environment. Develop collective intelligence. Know how to let go. Encourage cognitive diversity.

**The response**: foster trust and confidence in your organisation by asking two questions.

- How can I encourage teams to become more autonomous?

- How can I encourage the development of collective intelligence?

## Collaboration is in the nature of things

Collaboration is an integral part of nature. For example, we now know that trees communicate with each other and help each other out. When one tree lacks nutrients, other trees exchange them, particularly through their roots. When a danger to tree survival arises, information is passed on to trees far removed from the danger, and joint defence strategies are implemented.

Trees also collaborate with microfungi. The latter spread their filaments in the soil, providing the tree with much better hydration. In return, the tree supplies sugars to the fungi. A superbly orchestrated collaboration, but without a conductor.

Parallels can be drawn from these collaborative phenomena for human organisations. We'll come back to the conditions for the emergence of collective intelligence and the role of leaders in this context, but we can already say that within any human group there is an opportunity to disseminate a common intelligence that evolves collectively, enriches itself faster and better than solo or in silos, and surpasses in value the sum of individual intelligences. Even the most brilliant brain benefits from collective intelligence.

The designers of crypto currencies have certainly been inspired by the world of living beings. These currencies are in their infancy. They are only just beginning to be used as storage assets, and have not yet acquired the stability and track record of a traditional currency their status as money. For the rest, they rely on all the essential characteristics of a currency (durability, portability, fungibility, divisibility, scarcity etc). They offer the advantage of speed and they escape centralised control, at least so far, because they depend on an intelligent network of autonomous elements which, like trees, communicate within themselves. The phenomenon is set to accelerate with the emergence of protocols, enabling different currencies to interact with each other at lightning speed. So, in theory, it becomes possible to exchange bitcoin for ethereum, for example.

When applied to human groups, unfettered exchanges between individual intelligences can create a superior collective intelligence, thus optimising and accelerating value creation. It is on these precepts that agile organisational modes have developed. Initially in the digital field, before spreading with varying degrees of success to other sectors and professions. When these types of organisation falter, it is not so much the principle of collective intelligence and unfettered collaboration that is in question, but rather its modes of application, which are still the subject of experimentation today.

So, back to our leader. While we await a future world in which leaders may become obsolete, we may well ask ourselves what value they can add or, at least, how they can contribute to the development of collective intelligence, rather than hindering it, sometimes despite themselves. Perhaps this will become the key role of the leader: to energise collective intelligence, to identify blockages and help remedy them. A bit like my osteopath who uses a series of manual techniques to release blockages and initiate a whole-body rebalancing process that can last several days after the manipulation.

A few years ago, Belgium experienced an unprecedented situation, breaking the world record for the longest period without a federal government. At the time, despite this situation, it outperformed its neighbours in economic terms. As an American woman living in Belgium told me at the time: 'frankly, I didn't see any difference. Trains were running, rubbish was being cleared, the economy was running, wages were being paid, the sick were being cared for'.

To be fair, the country wasn't entirely without government, since it was run by the outgoing federal government and regional governments, in charge of many competencies, were also in place. Moreover, the experiment was taking place in a country that is by nature decentralised, where many systems have long been operating effectively and with a high degree of autonomy. Nonetheless, during my frequent travels at the time, I noticed that many outside observers found the experiment fascinating and wondered about the real added value of government. A kind of full-scale test of libertarian organisation. But, clearly, there was a collective intelligence in action and it proved to work with little leadership intervention.

It posed the question of the added value of leaders at the top. It is worth regularly rethinking their role from the perspective of optimising added value. If we agree that they must encourage and maximise collective intelligence, we need to identify potential obstacles. There may be many reasons why collective intelligence doesn't work well: nervousness and mistrust on the part of shareholders or owners; a poor spirit of collaboration; inadequate processes; undefined or ill-defined roles and responsibilities; psychological insecurity; operating in silos; lack of feedback loops; lack of cognitive diversity; a lack of motivation and sense of responsibility.

Let's imagine the leader in his role as facilitator of an intelligent collective system. One of the essential qualities expected is the ability to trust. Trust in the system, in people and in the nature of collective intelligence. Distrust is the leader's greatest enemy and the greatest enemy of organisations. For the leader, it is a question of practising the ability to trust and to facilitate the implementation of elements that will enable collective intelligence to function optimally with the greatest possible autonomy, rather than rigidifying the system and becoming a bottleneck. Let's explore this further with two questions.

## Question 17: how can I encourage teams to become more autonomous?

Organisations are comprised of six main components that interact with each other to generate value. They must reconcile two fundamental and contradictory requirements: to divide work into multiple tasks and to coordinate these tasks. A strategic summit (top management, executive committee etc) is responsible for achieving the organisation's mission, allocating resources and ensuring organisational efficiency. This top level is supervised by a non-executive body (board of directors, government etc) to which it is accountable.

Line management ensures the smooth running of operations within its scope, as defined by the summit. The operational centre carries out the organisation's mission and reports to line management. The technostructure (process and system optimisation) acts where there is interdependence. It ensures that interactions are optimised through norms, methods, standards and procedures. Logistics operates independently of the operational centre, but its purpose is to support it. It is often threatened by outsourcing. This structure can be found in each autonomous entity, for example, a geographical unit, which then reproduces it at its own level.

The leitmotif of each unit differs and can be summed up in a few words:

- For the strategic summit: 'control, control'.

- For the non-executives: 'show us the results, prove to us that it will work'.

- For line management: 'we are different from others, we have specific needs'.

- For operations: 'let us work our way'.

- For the technostructure: 'we must standardise'.

- For logistics: 'no waves, let's make ourselves essential, otherwise we risk outsourcing'.

All organisations, public or private, reproduce much the same pattern. You will no doubt have recognised the organisation in which you operate and the role you play within it. To apply the principle of optimising collective intelligence and empowering your teams, you need to delegate, which implies trusting, letting go and ensuring that objectives are set, roles and responsibilities are shared. In this process, you can involve your teams right from the stage of defining objectives, roles and methods, depending on their level of experience and self-confidence. Your role as coach or mentor will come into its own here. However, the balance needs to be reassessed regularly.

Too much autonomy and trust can destabilise teams, creating insecurity and frustrating employees who expect more support and help from you. Too much control and intervention, on the other hand, can demotivate, create dependency, breed followers, passive rebels and active rebels, depriving you of ideas you might otherwise have missed. It's essential to assess the maturity level of your teams and their members.

When composing teams, cognitive diversity has a well-established impact on performance, so it is worth paying close attention to it when selecting talent. The aim is to ensure that experience and skills, as well as operating and communication styles, complement each other. A precise definition of the skills required avoids the trap of recruiting similar profiles. The risk is even greater when it comes to personality style.

Let's return to the notion of delegation and empowerment. There might be differences between the two, but here we use them interchangeably. To put it simply, they are about using and developing collective intelligence in the service of an objective or mission.

There are many ways of delegating, depending on the situation, the skills, resources and time available, the potential of each individual and the objective to be achieved. In this respect, I have observed the following seven delegation faux pas, which I share with you here:

- Delegate for the sole purpose of getting rid of something you don't want to do.

- Delegating to individuals only to divide and retain control, rather than delegating collectively.

- Delegate, then disappear. Absence can send a signal that the work being done is not your primary concern.

- Nervous, tactical delegation. Too much control or spontaneous intervention, guided by your own stress.

- Delegate at the last minute because you wanted to keep control and suddenly realised you couldn't do it in time.

- Delegating without coaching: the aim of delegation is not simply to distribute work, but to develop skills.

- Delegate without a filter: delegating tasks and stress without restraint, rather than filtering out the right amount of stress needed to complete tasks with the right level of energy.

Delegation is an art that reflects the quality of leadership. Think about your organisation and your role.

- From a systemic point of view, where do you see yourself today: non-executive, strategic summit, line management, technostructure, operational centre or logistics?

- What does it mean to you?

- Are you satisfied with the way things are going?

- How do you assess the degree of trust you feel and demonstrate towards your stakeholders?

- And your own staff?

- How would you assess the balance between trust and control?

- What is your responsibility and what can you do to optimise team autonomy?

- What do the seven faux pas of delegation mean to you? or can you steer clear of them?

## Question 18: how can I encourage the development of collective intelligence?

In addition to delegation and empowerment, there are other principles that promote the proper functioning of collective intelligence, based on leaders' ability to build trust. Basically, four conditions must be met: cognitive diversity, independence of spirit, decentralisation and a clearly established governance model.

- **Cognitive diversity (or diversity of opinion)**: as important in the talent acquisition phase, as it is for promotions, deployments or team building. The trust factor must guard against the temptation to operate in closed circles and insider clubs. Empowerment will also lead to the emergence and reinforcement of diverse opinions based on different experiences. We also need to think about the systems and processes that will enable this diversity to be expressed and confronted.

- **Independence of mind:** an indispensable ally of cognitive diversity. Indeed, diverse opinions must be able to diverge without fear of condemnation from the top. You can't prevent the formation of contrary opinions; you can only silence them. Admittedly, this prospect can sometimes tempt the dictator in all of us. But if we want to become more intelligent and agile, it is important to create a culture conducive to debate and independent thinking. We need to create psychological safety to encourage teams to think freely and differently, feeling sufficiently supported in their diversity to dare to express themselves openly. It is a question not only of encouraging such a culture, but also of becoming its embodiment.

  What are we to think of a leader who feigns openness and willingness to listen, but loses his cool and loses his temper at the slightest sign of opposition? The ultimate goal is to enrich and fluidify exchanges, but also to ensure feedback. The practice of power can quickly become a solitary exercise, where the leader is surrounded by yes-men and where the feedback they receive, if any, is fragmented, watered down or even transformed. The challenge is not so much to be informed because you're the boss, but to be able to fully play your role as facilitator, decision-maker, referee and challenger.

- **Decentralisation:** essential to a system's flexibility, fluidity and speed of exchange and reaction. Of course, it must be accompanied by a system of governance that avoids paralysis or the dilution of responsibilities. But well thought out, this mode of organisation is the one that most closely resembles the living world. A digestive system doesn't need a brain to function fortunately. Each cell in the system plays its role autonomously. In fact, this is the prevailing model in many organisations. In this environment, the leader must trust the system or set up a system that fosters trust, taking care not to step outside their defined role and micromanage. Conversely, they must intervene at key moments and passages and be present as required. Leaders are an integral part of a decentralised system and their dysfunctions are just as likely to jam the mechanism as any other cog.

- **Governance**: complete the picture by clearly establishing the rules of operation and decision-making. To adapt the famous line by the pioneer of total quality management, W. Edwards Deming, 'in god we trust, all others must bring data', I would say, 'we trust in collective intelligence, all others must respect governance'.

If cognitive diversity, independence of mind, decentralisation and a clearly established governance model are the essential cogs in an effective system, and if trust is its basic software, listening and feedback are its lubricants. Without them, the cogs jam quickly.

*Listening*

We all know the adage: you have two ears and one mouth, so you listen twice as much as you talk. But what about in practice? Good listening, otherwise known as optimal listening or active listening, rest on three pillars: intention, attention and context.

- **Intention**: my intention must be to understand, to show genuine interest in understanding the other person's point of view. First, because I am interested in perspectives other than my own or those of my more usual circles. Everyone is an antenna and I can't necessarily pick up everything on my own. Secondly, the same signal will be picked up differently by someone else and it is interesting to understand a different perspective on something I may know but necessarily perceive differently. Thirdly, even if I am not sure I'll get any benefit from it, by listening to someone, you contribute to crediting the relationship account and encourage them to continue expressing themselves. If my intention is only to listen to contradict, argue or condemn, the exercise is biased. Of course, nothing prevents me from arguing and convincing to the contrary. But the more we decouple our reaction from listening, the more credible we are in the exercise, and the more likely we are to be surprised and benefit from other perspectives. So, first reflex: is my intention the right one? If it is, go ahead. If not, wait it out.

- **Attention**: when I listen to someone, that person is the most important person in the world for the few seconds or minutes I am listening. You don't need to do a lot of listening exercises to learn to maintain eye contact, to avoid looking at your screen while answering or jumping on the phone as soon as it rings, as if it were a welcome relief or distraction. Nor do you need to learn how to nod and maintain an attentive attitude. In this respect, what goes around comes around. When you want to be attentive, you are, and you can see and feel it. Keep this word in mind throughout the listening process: paying attention.

- **Context**: we all need to get a message across, sometimes a difficult one. We want to bring about a change in behaviour. The impulse is to jump at the first opportunity, vent our frustrations on the person and end the message with a strong injunction. Let's face it, it is a relief at the time and makes you feel all powerful. When you pull yourself together, you realise that this wasn't the best way to get your message across. It is actually better to listen to what the person has to say about the situation, their situation, which we need to hear before jumping to conclusions. This listening will enable us, first, to make sure that the real situation is indeed as we have perceived or imagined it and, second, to take the person on a journey of reflection that will enable them to decide on the change. In this process, we've thought about our intention and prepared ourselves to pay attention. Context is the last check. In other words, the right time and place to listen.

Let's reverse the roles for a moment: someone wants to talk to you. They want to ask you a few questions. Right now. You're in the middle of a stressful situation. You've got an emergency to deal with. What's your state of mind? What's your energy level? Are you ready for a discussion? Many years ago, I received a text message from an executive in the company where I was working at the time. A new leader I didn't yet know. At the beginning of the weekend. 'Could you call me as soon as possible? when would you have a moment this weekend?'

I decided to do what I do regularly, which is not to react on the spur of the moment, but to choose a moment when I was most likely to have the energy and attention required to listen fully. I sincerely thought that such a message in the middle of the weekend from a new leader did not augur well. So, I decided to make the most of one last good weekend and give it my full attention at 6 pm on Sunday. In the end, the gentleman offered me a promotion to my great surprise. Never assume. Thinking about context means choosing the right time and place to ask questions and getting into listening mode.

There are five levels of listening, and it is useful to remember them for every listening exercise.

- Listen to find the flaw in the other person's argument and better counterargue.

- Listen to provide a better response.

These first two levels are useful, but they don't in themselves constitute true, deep, authentic listening.

- Listen to understand, the level most frequently used by the leader.

- Listen to help the other person better understand their own thinking, the level used in coaching.

- Listen without an agenda. It is an exercise in presence and self-giving, the level I strive for when I visit my mother on Sundays, for example: a chosen moment in a context identified as conducive, when I make myself entirely available to her through my unconditional presence. It would be impossible for me to have the same level of attentiveness on a weekday evening over the phone. My attention span would not be optimal and my mental energy would not be sufficient to defuse all my impulsive reactions.

Creating the right context also means starting the dialogue with the right questions. It has been said that there are no wrong answers, only wrong questions. As Albert Einstein remarked: 'if I had one hour to solve a problem and my life depended on the solution, I would spend the first 55 minutes determining the right question, once I knew the right question, I could solve the problem in less than five minutes'.

Like active listening, asking the right questions rests on three pillars: intention, form and context.

- **Intention**: questions can be asked with three different or complementary intentions: to understand without preconceptions, to help thinking or to prompt someone to take a stand or decide. If I say: explain the situation to me, what's going on? Whether I already have an explanation or not, my intention is to listen without preconceived ideas to make sure I understand. If I say: how do you plan to do this? I want to help people think and find their own solutions. This is the basis of coaching. If I say: are you ready? I push the person to conclude. It stops the thinking process.

- **Form**: depending on my intention and the impact I want to produce, I'll then decide on the form of my question: whether it is open, as in the first two cases, or closed, as in the third. If I say, 'don't you think you could do it like that' (closed question), my real intention is not to understand the other person or make them think, but to get them to accept or reject my proposal disguised as a question.

- **Context**: as with listening, it is important to choose the most appropriate context in which to engage in dialogue.

*Feedback*

An organisation cannot function effectively without feedback. Feedback is the mirror effect. The response to the stimulus. When, as a child, I tugged at my sister's pigtails – nobody's blameless – and she cried ouch, I knew that my action was effective in terms of my intention, ie, to have fun while annoying her a little. If I pulled too hard, she'd scream, cry and I'd get reprimanded. I then distanced myself until the storm had passed. If she cried for a long time, I sometimes felt remorse and tried to make amends with positive gestures. If she didn't react, I was tempted to try again, pulling harder, or to move on to another game.

In a way, her feedback determined my attitude. When you're in a leadership position, putting your heart and soul into a mission, you need reactions and feedback, both when things go wrong and when they go right. At an organisational level, it is the sum of feedback that will enable us to confirm or modify the course of action at all levels.

When we don't take the trouble to give feedback, because of lack of time, indifference or fear of trouble, we deprive the organisation or teams of the signals needed for continuous improvement. Studies have shown that among the hundred or so levers that exist to boost performance within an organisation, feedback is one of the factors most correlated with improved performance. Promoting a culture of authentic feedback is therefore one of the obligations of any self-respecting leader. It involves creating an environment where people feel motivated and empowered to give feedback, and open and confident enough to receive it. To reduce feedback to an equation, a respectful, courageous and effective feedback culture is based on four criteria: intention, will, description and incentive.

- **Intention**: why do I want to provide feedback? what is the purpose? The intention of the giver ultimately is to help and the intention of the receiver to understand in order to continue to act as usual or to improve.

- **Will**: the donor's desire to help the person, the team or the organisation; and the receiver's desire to receive feedback and to receive it from that particular person at that particular time. When you're about to give (or ask for) feedback, it is a good idea to ask whether the person is open to receiving (or giving) feedback.

- **Description**: feedback consists in describing an observed situation, observed facts, verified behaviours, and, possibly, a personal perception. For example, you increased your productivity by 10 percent; or you interrupted your interlocutor several times during the meeting; or I found your speech a little slow for my taste and I found it hard to stay focused. You'll notice that this feedback is more likely to be heard with the right intention and with a shared will.

- **Incentive**: the purpose of feedback is to encourage the continuation of something effective or positive, or the improvement of something ineffective or negative. To achieve this, give a description of the consequences, for example, I had trouble staying focused. The idea is to present a situation and the cause-and-effect link between it and the result. Feedback can also be accompanied by a suggestion (sometimes called a feedforward), for example: 'I'd suggest that you speak a little faster or speed up certain passages that you've mastered well and pause on other elements to set the pace'. The bottom line is to avoid ending up with a description and no incentive.

The quality of feedback loses all its substance if either the giver or the receiver feels trapped. The giver must feel comfortable enough to end the discussion without having to apologise or justify. They offer feedback as a gift. The receiver is mature enough to decide what to do with it. Similarly, they feel able to clarify the feedback and to end the discussion by thanking the giver without feeling obliged to propose solutions or accept fault.

**Conclusion**

Thinking about your organisation or your teams:

- How would you assess the conditions for effective collective intelligence?

- What about cognitive diversity?

- The independence of spirit of its actors?

- Levels of autonomy?

- Governance and clarity of roles and responsibilities, particularly regarding decision making?

- What about the feedback culture? is it working optimally?

- What about your listening and questioning skills?

- What can you do to promote listening and feedback within your teams and organisation?

An effective, motivating organisation or team functions like a living body, whose components interact fluidly, with as few hindrances as possible. It owes its efficiency to the collective intelligence that determines its functioning and at the same time is enriched by it.

The role of the leader in this context is to ensure that the system works, that it breathes. They must prevent bottlenecks from forming. Like an orchestra conductor, the leader sets the pace and the orchestra does the rest. They do not impose anything, but their presence reinforces the whole. This requires perfect symbiosis. The orchestra must have complete confidence in its leader and in each member. The leader, for his part, must trust their orchestra.

This trust is the result of long-term work, numerous group rehearsals and the hard work of hand-picked individuals. So, it is not simply a matter of blind trust. Yet being a conductor is also an act of faith. It is not possible to become a good conductor without an unconditional trust in the ability of the musicians, whoever they may be, to produce superb collective work. The musicians themselves are unlikely to excel with a conductor who is mistrustful, overdirective or, on the contrary, indifferent. Confidence is a subtle combination of faith in teams, the courage and humility to stand back, and the foresight and audacity to intervene wisely.

# 7

# EXHAUSTION

*'Don't sacrifice too much, because if you sacrifice too much, you won't be able to give anything else and no one will be interested in you anymore.'*

**Karl Lagerfeld, fashion designer**

*'Taking care of yourself means giving the world the best of you, rather than what's left of it.'*

**Katie Reed, US writer, speaker and mental health advocate**

# EXHAUSTION

**The challenge**: ensure continuous regeneration for harmonious and sustainable individual, collective and organisational development.

**The risk**: exhausting yourself, exhausting others, failing to anticipate burn-out, failing to prepare the next generation, failing to develop talent, driving it away, underutilising potential.

**The opportunity**: contribute to regeneration, foster a growth mindset, prepare future generations, coach, mentor, manage own resources optimally.

**The response**: two questions to strengthen your powers of regeneration.

- How can I generate talent and invest in the future development of the collective?

- How can I develop personal regeneration routines?

## To live is to grow, to shrink is to die

A few years ago, I had the pleasure of exploring organisational systems: a fascinating look at the dynamics inherent in all types of organisation and their parallel with the living world. One of the fundamental precepts that struck me at the time was that all living organisms are driven by a single purpose: to grow. There is no status quo in the living world. It develops inexorably, seeking to occupy more space, to grow stronger and more numerous. The alternative is decline, disappearance and extinction.

Humans are no exception to this rule and destiny. We grow, seek to strengthen ourselves, occupy space, expand, and, when we reach our peak, we slowly decline, trying everything we can to slow it down. Until the inexorable extinction.

This discipline asserts that human organisations respond to the same logic, whether they are companies, institutions or states. They are all driven by this force that pushes them to expand. The only limit to this growth is the space available or the space occupied by others. Each seeks to expand according to its own strengths and must deal with the strengths of the other, whether territorial, military, demographic, economic or cultural. The frontier between two forces creates a need for cohabitation and collaboration and offers a space for co-development. When this cohabitation is well accepted, it creates a space of peace and mutual enrichment. Otherwise, it leads to discomfort, tension, disagreement, anxiety and, at worst, open conflict, leading to the exhaustion of resources. Think of couples, families, neighbours, colleagues, markets, organisations or nations.

Every leader or aspiring leader needs to take this reality into account on two levels: on a personal level, to manage their potential and their resources intelligently; and at the level of their area of responsibility, whether it is a team, a project, a department or an entire organisation, to ensure that they obtain, optimise, mobilise, develop and regenerate the potential they have or will need.

In this respect, the leader must combine three dimensions that fit together to create a virtuous dynamic within the collective under their responsibility. Correctly balanced, they generate a strong dynamic. Otherwise, they create potentially value-destroying distortions. This balancing mechanism acts like a battery on an electric vehicle. It powers the motor that turns the wheels. In turn, their rotation regenerates the battery. The same applies to the leader, whose optimal combination of the three dimensions feeds the collective, whose virtuous functioning energises the leader. These three dimensions are:

- The personal dimension: me.

- The collective or organisational dimension: we.

- The dimension relating to the object, the overarching purpose: it.

The leader must constantly balance these three dimensions. A leader who is too focused on me risks missing the objective (it) by being obsessed with their own self-interest. They make little effort to engage others (we) or do so in a manipulative way without regard for the interests or motivation of others.

A leader who is too focused on we can become absorbed by the need for energy and attention from those around them, losing sight of the end goal and their own interests. It is difficult for them to go against the collective and to make a decision in the event of divergence.

A leader obsessed with it can forget themselves, lose themselves and needlessly sacrifice their teams to achieve their goal, whatever the cost. They have trouble thinking about anything other than their objective. They underestimate the power of the collective and the impact of emotions in a group dynamic. They tend to neglect themselves and sacrifice themselves for the objective.

Obviously, there is no miracle formula in this area and the optimal balance will depend on circumstances. The ups and downs of a project, a career or a life may call for successive adjustments. However, I have also seen executives derailed by excessive imbalances. Here are a few cases I have observed.

- **The egocentric leader (me):** with a narcissistic streak, their personal success is their sole objective. Although there is no shortage of such people in our society, we can't really call them leaders. To take your first steps as a leader, you need to have shown a minimum of interest in we and it.

- **The clannish leader (me/we)**: an inflated ego, as we've already mentioned, isn't a problem, if it is tempered by genuine generosity and the desire to unite a team around yourself to serve your personal cause, whether or not it is in line with the broader objective of the collective. In this case, the leader is blinded by their own cause and has difficulty placing their objective in a wider perspective. They find it hard to stand back, perceiving any resistance to their project as a rejection or misunderstanding on the part of the collective. They expect their direct teams to fully support their objective. In return, they offer protection to their loyal followers.

- **The titanic leader (me/it)**: their need for power is matched only by the strength of the collective goal that drives them. They throw themselves wholeheartedly into a common cause. They find it an enormous source of motivation and an excellent way to shine and display their superior qualities. Other people are seen at best as a means to an end and at worst as a necessary evil, an adjustable variable or a resource to be manipulated and sacrificed.

- **The dedicated leader (it)**: willing to make any sacrifice, whether by themself or by others, to achieve the collective goal. They are often determined, enduring, humble and generous, and find it hard to understand that not everyone works as hard as they do. They totally ignore their own personal needs and find it hard to consider those of others.

- **The chivalric leader (we/it)**: like the dedicated leader, they fight body and soul to achieve the collective goal, while paying great attention to the motivation and wellbeing of their teams, for which they vouch, often excessively, and forgetting themselves completely. They may lack personal convictions, often aligned with the higher cause without discernment or the ability to stand back.

- **The altruistic leader (we)**: this leader's primary objective is the harmony and fulfilment of their teams. This excessive focus on the we prevents them from taking the necessary, sometimes unpopular, measures to get their teams (back) on track. They often lack internal conviction and find it difficult to establish their legitimacy as a leader and to make decisions in the event of disagreement or difficulties. Their focus on others can also cause them to lose sight of the end goal and their own needs.

These personas are, of course, caricatures. Everyone, I am sure, will have recognised certain characteristics of the leaders around them or perhaps detected some personal imbalances of their own. Let's explore how balanced leadership can mobilise, optimise and renew available resources.

## Question 19: how can I generate talent and invest in the future development of the collective?

The World Economic Forum has identified talent management as a rising competency that will be indispensable in the years to come. We all know how difficult it is for companies and institutions to find and attract new employees in all their diversity. A good corporate image and an effective recruitment policy are no longer sufficient. We need to know how to retain talent in the broadest sense of the term, motivate it, and detect the potential within our organisations that is just waiting to grow and develop. This is where the quality of leadership kicks in. Five factors combine to create an environment conducive to the development of potential:

- An organisational culture that encourages responsibility and autonomy.

- A genuine talent management policy that combines employer branding, active and strategic recruitment policies, and development opportunities with new challenges.

- Leadership practices based on clear, consistent principles, such as transparency, the right to make mistakes, continuous feedback and trust.

- Ongoing training with coherent programmes that adapt to the changing environment and promote the skills and behaviours expected, consistent with the culture and guiding principles of leadership.

- Innovative, flexible policies for performance management, compensation and benefits.

This systemic approach must not overshadow the responsibility of exemplary leadership. No talent management policy can succeed without it. In this respect, the strength of the chain is equivalent to the strength of the weakest link. A single leader acting as a counterexample is enough to undermine the best talent management policy.

*How do you scare off your best talent?*

Here are a few random examples that I have observed directly or indirectly over the past twelve months in organisations ranging from the most modest to the most prestigious in several countries on different continents. Fasten your seatbelts.

- A senior leader faced with a middle manager who was worried that the project he oversaw was coming to an end: 'consider yourself lucky to have a job'. I am not making this up.

- To a young talent, hypermotivated and dedicated, who falls ill a day after his colleague and whose manager responds: 'oh no, not two at the same time'.

- A general manager to whom I pointed out that he had absented himself, without warning, from a meeting that he himself had called, inviting his teams to come up with new ideas: 'my teams know that I was absent for a compelling reason', before adding, faced with my puzzled reaction: 'it is true that I can't stand it when people do that to me'.

- A general manager who decides to propose a new project manager to a customer, with whom he is close, and who announces to the customer that the initial candidate has withdrawn, a lie damaging to the reputation of that manager. A manoeuvre that did not escape the outraged and completely disengaged internal teams.

- A manager, who accepts an impossible deadline from a customer, throws the project into the hands of one of the team leaders, before going on vacation. On his return, he asks the team leader to review the project and, for reasons of personal preference, imposes a reworking of the completed work with three days to go. Only to conclude, one day before the deadline, that in the end he preferred the original version. All the while, the team leader, who had worked day and night on the project, looked on in dismay.

- A country director for a service company, who can't stand his staff overshadowing him, and does everything in his power to keep one of them away from a customer.

The result: individually he performs well, collectively, the country treads water. Many of the best talents are now working for competitors.

- An executive who, after an evening out with colleagues, finds himself in the same bedroom as one of them. As is often the way, the event reaches the ears of colleagues, who are torn between amazement, cynicism, contempt and amusement.

- A leader who asks excellent questions and is a superb listener, who then takes ownership of the content gathered and reaps the rewards later.

- A manager of a large organisation devises a Machiavellian plan to discredit a promising team member, because the latter has been highly recommended by a superior, close to the board, thus thwarting her initial intention to recruit an acquaintance. It took years of collective ostracism and exhaustion before discovering the cause.

- An executive in a major international institution draws up a plan to derail a transformation project that he had initiated, which was then piloted by another department. With the intention of eventually regaining responsibility for it, he ignored the impact on the organisation and the discredit brought to the project leader.

The list goes on. Unfortunately, the source is inexhaustible. These examples fall into two categories: on the one hand, behaviour that betrays a lack of ethics or malice on the part of its perpetrators, and, on the other, behaviour resulting from clumsiness, lack of competence or ignorance.

I won't dwell on the first category, whose resolution is more a matter of ethics or psychoanalysis. In the practice of coaching, we need to distinguish between the two quickly to ensure that we are indeed dealing with a question of lack of awareness, clumsiness or lack of skills. Ethics and values are probably the two most important criteria in recruitment, even before skills.

As a coach, I'll concentrate on the second category: clumsiness, lack of competence and ignorance. As a result of them or under the pressure of circumstances, we may act with good intentions, but provoke undesirable side-effects or even a totally opposite reaction. It's what we call inadvertent negative behaviour.

*Inadvertent negative behaviour*

A leader starts with good intentions. At first sight, all seems virtuous and likely to produce positive effects on motivation and climate and, therefore, on performance. However, counterproductive effects can happen. These negative behaviours are linked to a specific leadership style, which produces beneficial effects when practised wisely, but also perverse effects if care is not taken.

- **The perverse effects of visionary leadership**: too much vision kills vision. The visionary leader focuses on long-term objectives rather than immediate concerns. They inspire with a bold vision and give meaning to their teams. While it is generally accepted that visionary leadership has a highly beneficial effect on the collective, we must not lose sight of the side-effects of its excesses. A leader who is one step ahead of their teams can be perceived as too far removed from reality and not pragmatic enough. Busy with their strategic vision, they can give the impression of being uninterested in operational aspects, and, in so doing, unconsciously belittle the work of their colleagues. Their long-term optimism can disconnect them from the current concerns of their teams, making them less aware of risks, or discrediting them in the eyes of their teams who are exposed to concrete realities in the field.

- **The perverse effects of democratic leadership**: the democratic leader involves the teams in the design and implementation of the vision, strategy or action plans. This has a highly beneficial effect on teams, as well as on the quality and diversity of the ideas they generate. However, this approach can be counterproductive in more ways than one. At some point, decisions have to be made and compromises reached. If the leader doesn't intervene at the right moment, it can create confusion, doubt and demotivation. The manager must also calibrate the scope of their delegation. Either there is room for consultation and everyone is invited to share their suggestions or there isn't. The leader must then get their teams to express themselves on how to implement, rather than what they think of the decision, otherwise there is a risk of creating false expectations and generating frustration.

- **The perverse effects of coaching leadership**: the leader-coach takes a proactive, individualised approach to employee development, aimed at maximising potential and creating a positive, effective working environment. However, this approach also entails risks and undesirable effects. These include overdependence on the leader-coach, leading to a loss of autonomy in decision-making and self-regulation, or a considerable waste of time and energy resulting from inappropriate use of coaching when the employee resists change or has reached their level of incompetence.

- **The perverse effects of affiliative leadership**: this leadership style is based on individual support and empathy, making team members feel valued and understood. By emphasising harmonious interpersonal relationships, open communication and collaboration, affiliative leadership aims to create a sense of psychological safety within teams, which is conducive to innovation and productivity. However, excessive empathy on the part of the leader can prevent them from making objective decisions and lead to an overemphasis on recognition to the detriment of critical feedback. It can create a feeling of inequity, when they act too protectively towards some or pose as a saviour to the weakest, thus discouraging the best performers and the most enterprising. It can create confusion by saying yes to everyone or by avoiding taking a stand in situations requiring arbitration.

- **The perverse effects of authoritarian leadership**: authoritarian leadership rarely has a positive long-term effect. Nevertheless, it can be highly effective in certain crisis situations or when teams lack the maturity or skills to manage complex situations. Just as the absence of authority can have a negative impact on employees, an excess can have a deleterious effect on the prevailing climate. The go-ahead, strong-willed nature of the authoritarian leader may clash with the cautious, more analytical mindset of others. Employees may be subjected to unnecessary, even counterproductive stress. Fear of doing the wrong thing and paying the consequences can inhibit them, prompting them to pull out the umbrella at the slightest problem. Teams are paralysed without the continuous intervention of their leaders, slowing down performance and driving out the best people. Teams perform below their capabilities and their potential is underexploited.

- **The perverse effects of pacesetting leadership**: the conductor sets the tone, drawing the orchestra or teams into a dynamic from which it is difficult to escape without breaking the rhythm. Their intervention can help the collective to pick up the pace, moving from a waltz to a samba. They lead by example. But their boundless energy and exacting demands can exhaust teams, who then feel trapped in a narrow tunnel. Paradoxically, this leader shows the direction to be taken, but can give the impression of a loss of meaning and an absurd, frantic race against time. At worst, they put excessive pressure on team members to achieve unrealistic goals, contributing to excessive stress, disengagement and dropping out. Overenthusiasm can also lead them to monopolise the floor and have the answer to everything, thus inhibiting the creativity and autonomy of the team.

In the long run, these cumulative perverse effects drive away the most talented and ambitious, those who have the choice to leave and to change air. At a time when the war for talent is raging, it is far from a winning formula. To counter this negative spiral, the first step is to become aware of the responsibility of leaders for the lack of performance or the drain on talent. The worst performers can be unaware of their own responsibility. They see the problem, but don't realise they're part of it, like travellers who complain about overtourism in the places they visit.

Some understand their limitations but manage to disguise their poor leadership. They may be buoyed by a positive market, camouflage their average performance in the bigger scheme or blame poor performance on underperforming staff, whom they won't hesitate to sack and then replace, thus buying time until the hierarchy at the top changes. Sometimes their superior may be complicit in the manoeuvre because they like their direct collaborator and have a vested interest in maintaining the status quo and protecting the failing leader.

I don't want to paint a negative picture of the reality of human organisations, even if it's as old as the history of homo sapiens. For those wishing to raise the level of their leadership, I'd like to explore or remind you of a few avenues that might help you. Take out your development notebook and think about the following questions:

- How would you describe your balance between me, we and it? what about your managers and leaders?

- What about the five factors that contribute to the development of talent, and the regeneration of organisations and teams?

- What about the prevailing culture in your organisation? what are its positive aspects? are there any cultural elements that stand in the way of regeneration?

- How would you describe your organisation's talent management policy?

- What leadership practices are likely to attract, mobilise and develop the best talent? what happens in the event of underperformance?

- What about development and training opportunities?

- Do you see any perverse effects linked to your own leadership? what about the leadership of your managers and leaders?

- Is your system for performance management and compensation having a positive impact?

**Question 20: how can I develop personal regeneration routines?**

Our bodies are priceless resources. A few years ago, I was the victim of a type A aortic dissection (tearing of the aorta at the heart's outlet), a relatively rare phenomenon resulting in my case from a combination of genetic factors and excessive, prolonged stress, all the more insidious because I had so much fun in life and at work, and the stress in question was for me nothing more than adrenalin. So, I had the opportunity to physically feel the limits imposed by the body. More recently, slipping on a patch of ice, I fractured the malleolus of my right foot and a phalanx of my thumb. The result: an operation and two months' immobilisation. So, I speak from experience: our health is our most precious asset.

All this mobility in a healthy body is made possible by our three brains. They too deserve our attention. These brains are our three main centres of perception and information processing.

- **The head brain (or logical brain)**: it is located in the cerebral cortex and is associated with rational thinking, logic, analysis and decision-making. It processes information in a linear, factual way, using logic and objective data to solve problems.

- **The heart brain (or emotional brain)**: the heart is often symbolically associated with emotions, although these are governed by the limbic system in the head brain. This brain is the seat of emotions, feelings, empathy and intuition. It is sensitive to emotional signals, unconsciously influencing our responses and decisions.

- **The intestinal brain (or enteric brain)**: the enteric nervous system, located in the walls of the intestine, is sometimes called the second brain because of its importance for general wellbeing. It is closely linked to the central nervous system and communicates with it via the vagus nerve. This brain is involved in regulating the digestive system, but also plays a role in regulating emotions and psychological wellbeing. Recent research suggests that it may influence our moods and feelings.

For optimal mental and emotional health, all three of these brains are integrated into our thinking and decision-making processes. A holistic approach, which considers our rational thoughts, emotions and physical sensations, can lead to greater self-understanding and a more balanced life.

This complex mechanism, this set of organs controlled by a complex cerebral and nervous system, the body, housing our physical and mental faculties, is our only available capital. It is our best ally, but also potentially our worst enemy if we neglect it. Even if it is not (yet) immortal, it should be used as a renewable resource, not as a single-use fuel to be burned to the ground.

No leader worthy of the name can achieve great things without managing their body and mind as they manage their other resources. It is not necessarily a question of imposing an athlete's discipline, but of taking inspiration from it. I suggest you build your roadmap with the basics, your five sources of energy: physical exercise, your diet, your moments of rejuvenation, your social and emotional life, and your sleep.

*Physical exercise*

Movement is life. Prolonged immobility can have many adverse consequences on the body, such as muscle stiffness and loss of flexibility, muscle weakness, circulatory problems, increased risk of joint problems, bone degradation, reduced cardiovascular health, respiratory problems, reduced stamina and energy, digestive problems and an impact on mental health. So, it is vital to stay active and move regularly throughout the day, even if it is just by stretching or taking short walks. It is also advisable to maintain good posture and change position frequently if you have to sit or stand for long periods. Physiotherapists are seeing an influx of patients since the development of home working. Move, walk, stand up. Prefer the stairs to the elevator, public transport and walking to driving. Have a treadmill in front of your desk, an exercise bike in your office, a punch bag in the meeting room. Be creative, but move, change position.

There have been times on business trips when I've spent half an hour walking around my hotel room in front of one of the many indoor walking programmes, when conditions weren't conducive to exercise: unsafe neighbourhoods, lack of outdoor space, pollution, a crowded or too small a gym. Right now, I am writing while walking. I've acquired a desk that goes up and down electrically. It takes a while to get used to typing on the keyboard and concentrating while walking, but you get the hang of it. At a more advanced or professional stage, if you have the opportunity, do sport regularly, take on a sports coach or join a club.

*Your diet*

It is no secret that you become what you eat. The essential element above all others is water. Drink water. First thing in the morning: a large glass of water. Drinking a glass of water as soon as you get up has several health benefits, including helping hydration, boosting metabolism, supporting detoxification, improving digestion and increasing energy and concentration. It is a ritual I wouldn't break for the world.

As for the rest, I'll leave it up to everyone to define what suits them best. One of my customers eats once a day at 5 pm, others concentrate their mealtimes on eight hours and fast for 16 hours, and still others swear by this or that diet. I come from a country of gourmets, where beer, wine, excellent restaurants, Belgian fries, chocolates and waffles wage a frantic competition to win the favour of a conquered public. Fertile ground, then, for strengthening your willpower in the face of multiple temptations. Whatever the case, control what you eat and under what conditions. Consult a professional if you need to.

*Your moments of rejuvenation*

Our minds need a break. Recharging our batteries is essential for maintaining mental, emotional and physical balance. Here are a few ideas for recharging your batteries:

- **Meditation and mindfulness:** take a few minutes each day to meditate and practise mindfulness. It can help you calm your mind, reduce stress and reconnect with yourself.

- **Nature walks:** get outdoors and enjoy nature. A walk in a park, a hike in the mountains or a stroll by the sea can be refreshing and revitalising, such as the Japanese practice of *shrinrin-yoku*, forest bathing, which uses immersion in nature as a form of medicine. This technique has several health benefits: stress management, lower blood pressure, lower blood glucose levels, less fatigue, rejuvenation of mind and body, and a stronger immune system. *Shrinrin-yoku* has been part of Japan's national public health programme since 1982.

- **Physical exercise**: exercise regularly to release endorphins, the feel-good hormones. Whether it is practising yoga, running, swimming or any other physical activity you enjoy, moving your body can help you feel better about yourself.

- **Creative hobbies**: devote time to creative activities you are passionate about, such as painting, drawing, music, writing or cooking. These activities can be soothing and nourishing for the soul.

- **Practise gratitude**: get into the habit of writing down what you are grateful for every day, which can help you cultivate a sense of gratitude and focus on the positive aspects of your life.

- **Digital break**: take a break from using electronic devices for a certain amount of time each day. Step away from the screens and devote this time to activities that promote relaxation and human connection.

- **Self-care**: pamper yourself with wellness rituals such as relaxing baths, massages, at-home spa sessions or any other activity that helps you feel pampered and revitalised.

- **Positive socialisation**: spend time with supportive and inspiring friends and family. Sharing pleasant moments with loved ones can be a source of joy and comfort.

- **Reading and learning**: read inspiring books, interesting articles or listen to podcasts on subjects you're passionate about. Continuous learning can nourish your spirit and give you a sense of accomplishment.

- **Relaxation practice**: explore relaxation techniques such as deep breathing, yoga or listening to soothing music. These practices can help you release physical and mental tensions.

Find out what works best for you and incorporate these practices into your daily routine to recharge your batteries and feel revitalised. Above all, use this moment of rejuvenation as an opportunity to balance your life. If your job involves competition and speed, there's no need to throw yourself into a competitive sport. Respect your temperament and your desires, but also take it easy on yourself. It is all about managing your energies.

*Your social and emotional life*

It is often said that behind an individual's professional success lies a happy couple and a loving spouse. Emotional and social life play a crucial role in a leader's overall rejuvenation and wellbeing. In an age of technology and increasing social isolation, it is essential to understand and value authentic human relationships and meaningful social interactions.

Firstly, emotional relationships, be they family, friends or lovers, offer indispensable emotional support. They enable us to share experiences, joys and sorrows, creating a solid support network. This support is essential for overcoming the challenges and stresses of daily life, because it makes us feel understood, valued and loved. Moments of sharing and togetherness strengthen bonds and provide a sense of security and belonging.

Secondly, social interaction fosters personal development and fulfilment. They stimulate reflection, enrich perspectives and encourage open-mindedness. The diversity of exchanges with others enables us to discover new ideas, question our own convictions and grow as individuals. What's more, social activities such as group hobbies, discussions or collaborations provide opportunities for fun, relaxation and mental rejuvenation.

An emotional and social life is also essential for mental and physical health. Studies show that socially connected people are less likely to suffer from depression, anxiety and cardiovascular disease. Positive interactions release hormones such as oxytocin, which promote wellbeing and reduce stress. What's more, a strong social network can encourage healthy behaviours, such as regular exercise and a balanced diet.

Rejuvenation through social life is not limited to moments of conviviality, but also includes support during difficult times. The presence of friends and loved ones can help to overcome hardship, find solutions to problems and recover more quickly. Solidarity and mutual support strengthen bonds and reinforce the sense of belonging to a community.

Finally, emotional and social life helps to give meaning to life. Relationships with others enrich our existence, bringing moments of happiness and satisfaction, and enabling us to leave a positive mark on the lives of others. They give us a reason to get up every morning, challenge ourselves and contribute to a more harmonious world.

In short, emotional and social life is a fundamental pillar of healing. It offers emotional support, promotes personal fulfilment, improves mental and physical health, and enriches life with meaning and happiness. Cultivating and nurturing these relationships is essential to leading a balanced, fulfilling life.

In this respect, it is worth remembering the importance of the emotional account we have with our key relationships. We should approach our relationships with the idea of crediting the account as much as possible, not waiting until we need to debit it and certainly not enjoying the relationship as a pure consumer. A marketing director at a US retail company I have worked with, when asked what his recipe for success was, summed it up as follows: 'give, give, give without expecting anything in return'.

*Your sleep*

Good sleep has a profound and positive impact on performance, empathy and creativity. Let's explore how. Sleep is essential for memory consolidation and learning. During sleep, the brain processes and organises information acquired during the day, improving memory and recall. A good night's sleep improves concentration, alertness and the ability to solve complex problems. In addition, sleep promotes physical recovery, reducing fatigue and increasing endurance and physical performance.

Sleep also influences emotional skills, including empathy. Lack of sleep can impair emotional regulation, making individuals more irritable, less tolerant and less able to understand the emotions of others. On the other hand, adequate sleep enables us to better manage our own emotions and be more receptive to the emotions of others. This improvement in emotional regulation enhances the ability to empathise, show compassion and establish positive social relationships.

Creativity is closely linked to sleep quality. Sleep, particularly during REM (rapid eye movement), is crucial to creative processes. During REM sleep, the brain associates ideas in unconventional ways, which can lead to innovative solutions and original ideas. Good sleep also frees the mind from everyday worries, providing fertile ground for inspiration and creative thinking.

In short, good sleep is essential for optimising cognitive and physical performance, enhancing empathy and stimulating creativity. Good quality sleep enables the brain and body to function at their full potential, facilitating learning, emotional regulation and innovation. Cultivating healthy sleep habits should therefore be a priority for any leader or aspiring leader seeking to improve overall performance, nurture rewarding social relationships and foster creative thinking.

How about a siesta, as Winston Churchill used to do? He took a nap every afternoon, usually for an hour or two. He considered this break an essential part of his daily routine. He was convinced that this practice allowed him to recharge his batteries and work effectively well into the night. He felt that napping gave him a second day of work. The nap enabled him to clear his mind and maintain a high level of concentration and lucidity, helping him to cope with long working hours and stress.

Churchill encouraged his staff to adopt this habit. He declared: 'you must sleep somewhere between half an hour and two hours every afternoon. Then have a bath, a drink, a walk, and then, by all means, get back to work'.

Some companies are experimenting with napping by creating specially dedicated areas. In Saudi Arabia, some of my seminar participants take a micronap in their air-conditioned vehicle in the hotel basement. I give myself this gift whenever I can. To each his own. And if you have not taken one in a while, what are you waiting for?

## Conclusion

There can be no professional or personal performance and success without energy; and there can be no sustainable professional or personal performance and success without renewable energy. This is true at both individual and collective/organisational levels. We therefore need to approach energy management both tactically, through regular practices, and strategically over the longer term.

On an individual level, it all starts at the end of school. I observe this phenomenon in my daughters and nephews. As we enter the world of work, stress and fatigue at the end of the day or week increases. All-night parties are becoming increasingly expensive and that's when you become aware of your body's limits. I am not telling you anything new when I say that our body is a machine that wears out little by little. Like a battery that loses a little of its capacity every year. So, the need for self-care increases with time. Managing our bodies and minds must therefore be part of our strategy for career development and leadership optimisation.

Do you remember the first question we asked ourselves in chapter 1: who am I? An essential question, the driving force behind our existence and our actions. This driving force is lodged in our body: our self-awareness, the quality of our thoughts, our creativity, our openness to others and our ambition are all closely linked to our wellbeing, our health. '*Mens sana in corpore sano*', the famous quote from Juvenal's tenth satire, means 'a healthy mind in a healthy body'.

This need for sustainable development at individual level is also found at organisational level. In this respect, I'd like to share two recent examples.

A start-up that has grown by leaps and bounds: it is a real success story, the brainchild of an ambitious, highly intelligent young founder. Thanks to investments from business angels excited by the project and, above all, by the attractive growth prospects, the company grew rapidly.

That's the visible part of the story, as reported in the press. The other side is less glowing and has been told to me by people who have worked there. Autocratic leadership at the top and the absence or shortage of leadership among newly promoted managers create a climate of stress and mistrust which contributes to high staff turnover. It is nothing out of the ordinary and I have no doubts about this company's ability to do what it needs to do to ensure its sustainable development. There is a real market for leadership development in young organisations.

A fast-growing company in the sports sector: here too, regional managers who are not always well equipped to manage, sometimes unwittingly contribute to encouraging deleterious practices among the team leaders who report to them. The result? Take a guess. The best people leave. Regional managers cover for their team leaders, justifying turnover by a difficult and fickle talent market.

These two stories, which came to my attention as I was writing these last pages, lead me to two reflections. First, life is an eternal restart. After more than 35 years of a career devoted to the development of business, entrepreneurship, and leadership, I sometimes have the impression that everything I share is obvious and well known to everyone. These examples prove the contrary and rekindle my flame, because they demonstrate that quality leadership is a rare commodity and that its development is a work in progress.

Second, the dysfunctions I've been observing all this time are appearing at every level of the pyramid and in every cog in the constellation. Seniority or past success are no guarantee of irreproachable leadership. Constant vigilance and self-examination are essential.

# CONCLUSION: GROWTH PLAN

*'An idea that is not put into practice is a dead idea.'*

**Ernesto Sirolli, Italian**
**author and public speaker**

*'The secret to getting ahead is to get started.'*

**Mark Twain, US writer**
**and humourist**

One percent improvement a day is the key to your personal and professional success. Because if you do not evolve, change or continually improve, if you cling indiscriminately to the old recipes that have made you successful in the past, you risk becoming obsolete, but, above all, you deprive the world of the best in yourselves. Fate, nature or god, depending on your beliefs, has catapulted you onto this earth to accomplish a mission: to change the world, change your country, change your city, create a family or bring wellbeing to those around you. Whatever your level of ambition and impact, at your level you cannot stop halfway and operate on autopilot. You are capable of more, of better. Do not give up along the way. Develop your full leadership potential and change as often as you need to. Keep moving forward. And since the best way to move forward is to put one step in front of the other, I suggest you set up a continuous leadership improvement routine, or revive or maintain it, depending on your situation.

Before we get down to it, I would like to remind you of the philosophy we share as we gather round this book. A growth mindset based on the fundamental belief (a reinforcing belief) that abilities and talents are not innate and immutable, but can be developed through hard work, learning and perseverance. We are convinced that challenges and failures are opportunities for learning and development, and that effort and perseverance are essential means of developing skills. We welcome, even seek, constructive criticism as a means of improving ourselves. More than a belief, it is a value. Something fundamental that drives us, but also the model we project around us, and the world we strive to shape.

**Question 21: what is my growth plan?**

So where to start? Any collective or individual improvement process goes through two phases: divergent and convergent.

*The divergent phase*

During the divergent phase, we absorb like a sponge, exploring, reflecting and letting things settle. This book, the 21 questions and their many sub-questions are designed to shake up our certainties, provoke or accelerate our thinking. In this field, there are two types of personalities: maximisers and minimisers.

Maximisers are comfortable with the idea of leaving doors open, continuing their exploration without rushing, stirring up more ideas, with the aim of producing a fuller, richer synthesis in due course. Their challenge: to avoid lingering too long in the divergent phase, to avoid drowning in an excess of reflections and to focus on one point, the convergent phase.

Minimisers, on the other hand, are overwhelmed by the influx of information, and their reflex is to cut to the chase and jump to conclusions. Their challenge is to avoid jumping to hasty conclusions, missing out important elements, and to give things time.

A continuous development process, like leadership in general, calls for a fusion between maximising and minimising modes. Alternating divergence and convergence in regular, frequent back-and-forth movements.

*The convergent phase*

Then, in the convergent phase, follow this series of steps. First, summarise your thoughts at a given moment. I suggest you take all your notes on the questions and on the sub-questions raised in this book. After rereading, switch to minimiser mode and ask yourself the following summary questions.

- What have I discovered?

- What are my limiting attitudes in relation to my personal and professional goals?

- What are my reinforcing attitudes?

- What should I capitalise on?

- What do I need to improve or compensate for?

Take a maximum of three key points, or two, or even just one, on which you decide to focus for a limited period of time, like a sprint in agile mode (a few days, a few weeks or even a few months). For example, I want to improve my health and lose weight. For each of these, define a smart goal. To take our example: I want to lose five kilos in three months.

Now, to motivate yourself and ensure implementation, you're going to define a predictive performance indicator. Losing five kilos by a target date is a key performance indicator, but it is not predictive. It can only be measured once the result has been achieved or after a progression stage. But it is always reactive. Its achievement can only be observed after the effort has been made. Unlike the predictive indicator.

For example, if I know that reducing my daily calorie intake from 2200 to 1500 will certainly help me lose weight, I can use this as a predictive indicator. Choosing the right predictive indicator is the key to real progress.

That said, it is more difficult to implement because you have to choose an indicator that is truly predictive of what you want to achieve (you have to be sure that cutting calories will lead to weight loss) and over which you have real influence (you are able to control what you put on your plate), because it is more difficult to measure and monitor. Obviously, to lose weight, there are other elements that can contribute, such as sugar or fat intake, physical activity, meal frequency or timing, but the objective here is to select one, which, while not constituting the whole approach, will have the merit of focusing attention by its isolated and unique character.

This is all the truer if you want to boost the performance of a department or team for a certain period. Isolate an objective, identify one of several predictive indicators collectively and measure regularly and frequently. Please note that the above examples are purely indicative. Consult a professional if you wish to establish a plan tailored to your personal needs. It is obvious, but you know how things work these days.

Then implement and maintain your dashboard on a regular basis and evaluate progress. Once an objective is reached, repeat the process, starting with divergent, then convergent thinking. Keep the daily one percent in mind. I wish you a superb career and a wonderful life.

*'The best way to predict the future is to create it.'*

**Peter Drucker, management
writer and thinker**

# ACKNOWLEDGEMENTS

I would like to express my thanks to all those who helped to design, publish and distribute this book. The list is long and I would probably have to rewrite a whole book to retrace its entire genesis, because a book is the fruit of so many encounters and experiences, happy or not, pleasant or painful. Each of them has enabled me to progress as a human being, as a leader and as a professional.

I would also like to thank all those who have sincerely encouraged me at every stage of the book's publication to keep going. I would also like to thank my dearest ones who, through their presence and their authentic comments, have enabled me to write this book.

I would particularly like to thank those who helped me in the finishing line with their comments. I would like to mention: Odile Mohan, seasoned CRHO, who, after reading the draft of my book, gave me the final nudge I needed to decide to publish the book; Patrick Faniel, managing director of MCE (AMA) for his support and comments; and, last but not least, Adam Jolly, professional journalist and publisher, whose trust, professionalism and advice made it possible to localise, refine, publish and distribute this book.